T5-AFL-568

RELIGION IN ISRAEL TODAY

The Relationship Between State and Religion

RELIGION IN ISRAEL TODAY

The Relationship Between State and Religion

by

Joseph Badi

Bookman Associates
New York

BM
390
.B3

Copyright 1959, by Joseph Badi

Library of Congress Catalog Card Number: 59-14626

MANUFACTURED IN THE UNITED STATES OF AMERICA
PRINTED BY RECORD PRESS, NEW YORK, N. Y.

Dedicated

to

Jeremiah, the Prophet

Galileo Galilei
and
Baruch Spinoza

three non-conformists who fought and suffered
for their independence of thought

ACKNOWLEDGMENTS

I owe a debt of gratitude and appreciation to the following:

Dr. Hans Staudinger, Dean, Graduate Faculty of Political and Social Science; Dr. Arthur L. Swift, Jr., Dean, School of Politics and Social Studies; and Drs. Erich Hula, Otto Kirchheimer, Saul K. Padover, and Howard B. White, my professors in the Department of Political Science, Graduate Faculty, New School for Social Research, New York;

Dr. Horace M. Kallen, for his guidance and advice in publishing this book;

Mrs. Sylvia Landress, Director of the Zionist Archives and Library, New York, and to the librarians, for their generous assistance in obtaining all the documentary material;

Miss Sonia Volochova, for her editorial aid and technical assistance; and

My devoted wife, Irene, whose unfailing understanding and sympathetic encouragement enabled me to undertake and complete the publication of this work.

CONTENTS

INTRODUCTION

There is, in the Western world, a widespread misconception that the law of Israel is theocratic in both content and application. This work was undertaken in an effort to combat this misconception. As in the case of similarly misbegotten and dangerous fallacies, this theocratic myth is best exploded by exposure to the light of truth. The truth, in this case, is that the majority of Israel's people is struggling to achieve a modern democracy governed not by rabbis or rabbis' lay representatives but by the people's elected leaders; a democracy that will fulfill the promise of Israel's Declaration of Independence to "ensure complete equality of social and political rights to all its inhabitants irrespective of religion, race or sex."

Nor is this truth made less valid by the fact that, as they do throughout the world, the orthodox Jews in Israel voluntarily submit to ecclesiastical rather than secular law. Neither is it injured by such submission, for the best Jewish traditions are in accord with the highest principles of democracy.

There were, it is true, and there still are, powerful pressure groups which endeavor to foist religious law upon the new State. But the concessions, such as the legalization of the Saturday sabbath, gained by them do not make Israel a Jewish theocracy, any more than the Sunday sabbath makes the United States a Christian one. The Israeli legislature has time after time reaffirmed the principles of democratic government, that is, government according to the will of the majority.

This is not to say that Jewish consciousness has no effect upon Israeli law, either legislatively or judicially. In dealing with certain problems of interpretation of old statutes promulgated under Ottoman or Palestinian auspices, the Israeli courts have repeatedly been influenced by Jewish ethical standards. What Israel is really trying to do is to effect a synthesis between its Jewish cultural heritage and the requirements of a free modern democracy. It is worthy of note, however, that because Israel is a modern nation, Jewish tradition has no choice; it must, and does, take into consideration the needs and ethics of a free and progressive society. Raising the marriageable age of girls from fifteen to seventeen years, the Women's Equal Rights Law, the absolution of polygamy, corroborate this progressive orientation.

It should be clear to the open-minded reader that the modern state of Israel has adopted an eclectic approach to legal problems. Jewish tenets or traditions that are well-suited to a modern, progressive community, are readily incorporated into law; but Jewish precedents, no matter how long established, which in the light of modern practice appear unreasonable or inequitable are expected by the secular majority to be amended in favor of more progressive democratic decisions as called for by modern needs. The argument so often raised, not only in Israel but, as well, in communities adhering to other religious systems, that a law or tradition must remain inviolate because of its divine nature or origin is not accepted by Israel's secular majority.

In view of the foregoing, logic must lead the unbiased observer to conclude that, since Israeli law incorporates not alone the ethics of Jewish tradition but is marked, to an even greater extent, by democratic flexibility and practicability, the new State of Israel is building a modern democratic Western state and not a Middle Ages theocracy. Israel has, in fact, chosen democracy as a way of life not only because of claims that the concept is Jewish in origin, but because of democracy's applicability to the needs of modern political and economic development.

It is my hope that this book will help to clarify Western understanding of the essentially democratic nature of Israeli law. Such understanding, in a world increasingly embroiled in the conflict between totalitarian and democratic ideas, is indispensable to the future effectiveness of Israel's role as a bulwark of democracy in the Middle East.

JOSEPH BADI

Part I

HISTORICAL BACKGROUND

1. *The Jewish Religion in Antiquity*

The word "religion" is derived from the Latin *religio* (pious conduct). It means the respecting of values instituted in the past. *Dath,* the Hebrew word for "religion," means "law." In Esther we read—*dath va'din.*[1]

Every religion has its metaphysical origin. Common to the Jewish, Christian, and Islamic faiths is the belief in the unity of God.

There is, however, a primary difference between the Jewish and other religions. Other nations can be split into several religions. But according to the Mosaic conception, the terms "religion" and "nation" are inseparable and integral parts of the concept of Judaism.[2]

For a study of religion in the new State of Israel, one must pause and examine the history of Judaism in the Jewish Commonwealth of antiquity, its status in the medieval world, and the modern Zionist movement that brought the new Israel and its political parties into being.

Generally speaking, Judaism is not a religion in the usual sense of the term; it is rather a system of communal living. Herein lies the essential difference between Judaism and other monotheistic religions. Judaism is ethical teaching that encompasses community and society, whereas the other monotheisms are concerned with the spiritual problems of individuals. They want only to save the soul of the individual, whereas Judaism cannot compromise with a corrupt social order. It is concerned with wholeness in both the life of the individual and the life of society. Perhaps it is this social consciousness that explains why there are no schisms in Judaism, why the Mosaic teachings are not conducive to sectionalism. It may also explain why in other religions a schism nearly always involved a reaction against the older Church and seldom stemmed from a national civil dispute, whereas in Judaism religious heresy nearly always —especially in the ancient and medieval periods—involved a rejection of Jewish national identification. Spinoza is a case in point.[3]

2. *Religion as the Stronghold of the Jewish People in Exile*

If the first affirmation of Jewish faith is the sovereignty of the Living God, the second is the election and vocation of Israel. In the normative Biblical-Rabbinic view, Israel is not a "natural" nation; indeed, it is not a nation at all like the "nations of the world." It is a supernatural community called into being by God's special act of covenant—first with Abraham,[4] whom God "called" out of the heathen world, then, supremely, with Israel corporately at Sinai.[5] The covenant of election is what brought Israel into existence and keeps it in being. Apart from the covenant, Israel is as nothing and Jewish existence a mere delusion. The covenant is at the very heart of Jewish self-understanding of its own reality.

"You shall be unto me a kingdom of priests and an holy nation." [6] That is the basic formula in which the vocation of Israel is defined. Taken in its fullness, as it is developed in subsequent Biblical and Rabbinic thought, this commission may be seen as implying a triple task: to receive and cherish the Torah of God; to hear and obey His voice in loving service and thus to live a holy life in a holy community under His Kingship; and to be a "light to the gentiles." [7]

"In Israel all religion is history." [8] Jewish religion is not a system of propositions to be apprehended intellectually, or esoteric wisdom to be received in mystic illumination. Jewish religion is history, or rather it is faith enacted as history, not to be understood, experienced, or communicated apart from it. "History," Professor Baron tells us, "is the all-pervading dominant sanction for the most fundamental ideas of Jewish religion, including the concepts of Messianism, the chosen people, the covenant with God, and the Torah."[9] This history is the history of Israel, and of the world as related to Israel, interpreted from the point of view of God's redemptive purpose.[10]

One of the cardinal precepts of traditional Judaism is the Sabbath: "He rested on the seventh day from all His work which He hath made."[11] The Sabbath is also a social institution which stresses the equality of every person in Israel. "But the seventh day is a Sabbath unto the Lord thy God, in it thou shalt not do any manner of work—thou nor thy son, nor thy daughter, nor thy man-servant, nor thy maid-servant, nor thine ox, nor thine ass, nor any of thy cattle, nor thy stranger that is within thy gates—that thy man-servant and thy maid-servant may rest as well as thou."[12]

The continuing importance of this precept is illustrated by the point of view expressed by D. Z. Pinkas, late Israeli Minister of Communications and Mizrahi leader, at a debate at the Hebrew University (Jerusalem) Students' Union:

> In our day the Sabbath in Israel should retain its original form as laid down in the Torah and the Shulhan Arukh[13] in order to insure complete equality for all sections of the community. Any other kind of Sabbath would merely become a parody of the traditional day of rest; it would not grant complete and perfect rest to the entire population and would simply degenerate into a Jewish counterpart of the Christian Sunday—on which part of the population enjoys itself at the expense of the rest of the community. On Sunday, transport workers and employees in places of amusement and cafes actually work harder than during the rest of the week. This problem cannot be solved by giving these workers a day off during the week as a substitute for the Sabbath, since physical relaxation without spiritual repose cannot be considered a complete rest in the full sense of the word. A state of spiritual evaluation combined with joyous celebration—such as is attained by the traditional Sabbath—can only be accomplished by observing an all-inclusive day of rest which affects the entire community and not just part of it. A day off in the middle of the week, therefore, cannot grant the same feeling of complete spiritual

relaxation and rejoicing which are *sine qua non* of the Sabbath.[14]

3. *New Trends in the Jewish Religion in the Modern World*

In medieval times the Jews were as dispersed as they are today. The political and social conditions of the countries in which they resided influenced the development of their faith. The non-existence of a Jewish political state was especially instrumental in this development, for religion was the only "state" which united the Jewish people no matter where they lived. Religious leaders were national leaders as well, and severely punished all religious aberrations. Their word was law: *Cuius Regio Eius Religio*.[15] They ruled with the blessing of the secular state, which found such an arrangement convenient from both a fiscal and an administrative point of view.

The Jewish Middle Ages did not come to an end until 1789. With the Jewish emancipation from the ghetto came the Haskalah,[16] with such spokesmen as Mendelsohn.[17] Concomitantly, there appeared in Germany the Reform Judaism movement. This movement was essentially one of assimilation and was constrained only by the integrated character of East-European Jewry. It sought this assimilation through reforms of the Jewish prayerbook, ritual, etc. It therefore encountered the opposition of such religious leaders as Krochmall,[18] Luzatto,[19] and Pines and Yaavets,[20] and of such secularists, and even socialists, as Hess,[21] Pinsker,[22] and Lilienblum[23]—and finally, of Herzl[24] and his followers.

As a consequence of the failure of the Haskalah and Reform movements, and of the antisemitism preached by such "theorists" as Stoeckel,[25] and Chamberlain[26] and manifested in the Dreyfus trial[27] in France and in the organized pogroms[28] of Czarist Russia, there arose the Zionist movement which aimed at the settling of the Jewish people in Palestine; the establishment of a Jewish State; the renaissance of Hebrew as the language of the Jews; and the territorial concentration of the Jewish masses in Palestine. The movement embraced various political parties with various political viewpoints, from socialists to extreme religionists. It was therefore prudent for Zionism to remain completely neutral in religious affairs.[29] Religion was the concern of the individual party. This kept Zionism intact, but it resulted in dire consequences both before and after the establishment of the State of Israel.

4. *The Jewish Religion in Mandatory Palestine*

Immigration to Palestine began after the Russian pogroms of 1881. The pogroms transformed Jewish life—both national and social. The reaction against Czarist despotism and the corrupt social order woke nationalist and socialist sentiments in Jewish youth. It is little to be wondered at that—at a time when religion was "the opium of the people" [30] and the Czarist government used the Church as a tool (e.g., the demonstration with the priest Gapon which ended in a massacre instigated by provocateurs)[31]—Jewish youth should discard the traditions of their faith, or that the first Israeli pioneers were not religious and did not accept the authority of the Torah codes which had regulated Jewish life for so many centuries.

The new Jewish community in Palestine was completely secular. The religious Palestinian Jews of Safed, Hebron, Jerusalem (Meah She'arim), and Jaffa represented a world entirely different from its world. But after the Balfour Declaration of 1917,[32] the San Remo Conference of 1920,[33] and the British Mandate for Palestine confirmed by the League of Nations in 1922,[34] a new religious element came to Palestine. The British administration in Palestine gave the Jewish community internal autonomy, an internal communal organization (Knesset Israel), with an executive branch (Va'ad Le'umi), and the Chief Rabbinate. These had authority over all who voluntarily joined the Knesset Israel.[35] This enabled extremist religious groups, such as the Neturei Karta, to remain outside the organized community, and permitted the establishment of independent party-school systems. There was no internal focal point around which all religious schools and authorities could group. Such a point—according to Rabbi Yehuda Maimon, first Minister of Religious Affairs in Israel—was to be comprehended as a central authority, a Sanhedrin,[36] which would be decisive in all problems pertaining to religious law, for Rabbi Maimon believed that Israeli jurisprudence must be founded on traditional Jewish law. In his "Revival of the Sanhedrin in Our New State," he advances the following arguments:

> Without the Torah—without the restoration of its principles and its legal code—The State of Israel is like a body without a soul. . . . Such a tremendous task, the task of reconstituting our old law in our young state will call for the formation of a Sanhedrin. For the day is not far off when our state will be confronted with decisive problems rooted in the rebirth of our state in modern times and in an era of great technological progress. To properly balance the old with the new and meet adequately the modern conditions of life, a Sanhedrin—a body of seventy-one members, composed of those who are steeped in the wisdom of the Torah and those who are educated in modern sciences, is essential.[37]

The origins of the present religious situation in Israel date back to the pre-1917 period, when Palestine formed a part of the Turkish Empire. It was the policy of the Imperial Turkish government to delegate exclusive jurisdiction over matters of personal status to the courts of each religious group within its orbit. Under this policy, the Rabbinical Courts applied the law of Shulhan Arukh to all questions affecting the personal status of the Jews.

Under British rule, the courts of the various religious groups in Palestine retained a substantial part of their broad jurisdiction in the personal-realm status of their members.[38] But, in deference to the pressure exerted by liberal groups, the authority of the Rabbinical Courts was somewhat curtailed by the British Mandatory Government.[39] The 1922 Order in Council,[40] which remains one of Israel's most important laws, provided that the Rabbinical Courts exercise exclusive jurisdiction over all matters pertaining to marriage, divorce, alimony, and confirmation of wills arising among members of the Jewish community who were either citizens of Palestine or stateless people. Jurisdiction over all matters of personal status not involving the above was vested in the State District Courts. The exclusive jurisdiction of the Rabbinical Courts applied only to members of the Knesset Israel, which was the autonomous organization of Jews who were Palestine subjects.[41] But neither the Rabbinical nor the State District Courts had authority to grant divorces to, or nullify the marriages of, alien Jews residing in Palestine. As a result no alien of Palestine could obtain a divorce. Not until 1943 did the Supreme Court of Palestine rule that a Rabbinical Court could issue an order of divorce to alien Jews if both parties consented to accept its jurisdiction.

The complex and unsatisfactory situation in the sphere of personal law and jurisdiction which existed in Palestine on the eve of independence was inherited by the young State of Israel.[42]

According to the existing laws there is no appeal from a decision of the Supreme Rabbinical Court to the Civil Supreme Court. But the High Court of Justice can issue a writ prohibiting the Rabbinical Court from exercising jurisdiction over matters not within its authority. The Rabbinical Courts have no executing officers and a civil executing officer can, under certain circumstances, refuse to execute a rabbinical judgment.

A Special Tribunal may determine whether certain cases are in the competence of the Civil or the Rabbinical Courts. But no appeal to Civil Courts is possible in cases where jurisdiction has not been abused by the Rabbinical Court. All important national, social, and cultural problems, clearly divided public opinion, and varied cultural groups—from modern secular to medievally traditional and religious ones—demand, on the one hand, that all future Israeli legislation be based on the Law of the Torah, and on the other, that civil marriage and divorce systems be established.

The inevitable consequence was that few changes have been made, and these are compromises and not fundamental changes. The religious parties, for instance, accepted the National Service Law, but only after they were promised the exclusive competence of Rabbinical Courts in matters of marriage and divorce.[43]

The argument against civil marriage and divorce advanced by the religious is based on the contention that such a law would divide the nation in two and all intermarriage between orthodox and non-orthodox Jews would cease. To avoid a *Kulturkampf,* many supporters of civil marriage and divorce decided not to press their demands at present, and the Rabbinical Courts gained exclusive jurisdiction over all marriages and divorces of Jews, both citizens and non-citizen residents. The Rabbinical competence and jurisdiction exercised during the British Mandate was thus enlarged.

In other fields the religious groups were not as successful in their opposition to reform. New provisions made substantial changes in the existing Jewish Personal Law.

In 1951, the Knesset passed the Women's Equal Rights Law.[44] It gave women equal rights with men. This entitles them to full rights in the Rabbinical Courts and accords married women full property rights. These provisions change the traditional Jewish law of property relations between husband and wife, according to which the husband is entitled to the income from his wife's property. The law also provides that, in cases of divorce, the mother, and not the father alone, can be the children's guardian. According to Jewish traditional law only the father was entitled to guardianship.

Other provisions still further protect women's rights. A wife can now imprison a husband who refuses to divorce her—if the divorce has been ordered by a Rabbinical Court[45]—or a brother-in-law who refuses to give *halitsa.*[46]

It is difficult to foresee further developments in the personal status law. While minor reforms may be instituted in the near future, no major changes are likely to be effected in the Rabbinical competence over marriage and divorce.

NOTES: PART I

1 1:13 ". . . for so was the king's manner toward all that knew law and judgment."

2 D. Z. Pinkas, "Religion's Place in Israel," *Jewish Horizon*, XIV (November, 1951), 12-14.

3 Baruch Spinoza (1632-1677), a monist affirming there is but one substance or reality. In his *Tractatus* he was the first to apply scientific scholarship to the Bible.

4 Gen. 15:18.

5 Exod. 19:5.

6 *Ibid.* 19:6.

7 Isa. 42:6.

8 Martin Buber, *Hasidism* (New York: Philosophical Library, 1948), p. 199.

9 Salo Wittmayer Baron, *A Social and Religious History of the Jews* (New York: Columbia University Press, 1937), I, 7.

10 Will Herberg, "What is Jewish Religion?" *Jewish Frontier*, XVII (October, 1950), 8-13.

11 Gen. 2:2.

12 Deut. 1:14.

13 The Code of Rabbinical Law by Joseph Caro (1488-1575).

14 *Jewish Horizon*, XIV (November, 1951), 13.

15 A principle which followed the Thirty Years' War in Europe (1618-1648).

16 A Hebrew word meaning "intelligence" which was applied to the Jewish Enlightenment movement which began in Western Europe in the middle of the 18th century.

17 Moses Mendelsohn (1729-1786), Jewish philosopher, author, and translator of the Bible into German.

18 Nachman Krochmall (1785-1840), Jewish philosopher.

19 Shmuel David Luzatto (1800-1865), Jewish philosopher.

20 Zeew Yaavets (1848-1924) and Yehiel M. Pines (1842-1913), founders of the religious Zionist Mizrahi Party.

21 Moses Hess (1812-1875), author of *Rome und Jerusalem* (1862).

22 Leo Pinsker (1821-1891), author of *Auto-Emanzipation* (1882).

23 Moses L. Lilienblum (1843-1910), Russian Zionist.

24 Dr. Theodor Herzl (1860-1904), author of *Judenstaat* (1896) and founder of the modern World Zionist Organization.

25 Adolf Stoeckel (1835-1909), author of *Wach auf Evangelisches Volk* (1893).

26 Houston Stewart Chamberlain (1855-1927), author of *The Foundations of the Nineteenth Century* (1910).

27 Alfred Dreyfus (1859-1935), Jewish captain in the French Army, was falsely accused of treason, court-martialled, and condemned to Devil's Island.

28 Massacres of Jews.

29 Israel Cohen, *The Zionist Movement* (London: Frederick Muller, 1945), p. 71.

30 Karl Marx, "Zur Kritik der Hegelischen Rechts Philosophie," *Deutsch-Französische Jahrbucher* (Paris, 1844), pp. 71-85.

31 A demonstration of Russian workers led by the priest Gapon (1870-1906), January 9, 1905 ("Bloody Sunday") ended in a large number of victims.

32 Helen Miller Davis (ed.), *Constitutions, Laws, Treaties of States in the Near and Middle East* (Durham, N.C.: Duke University Press, 1953), p. 339.

33 *Documents Relating to the Palestine Problem* (London: Jewish Agency for Palestine, 1945), p. 7.

34 Davis, *op. cit.,* pp. 328-335.

35 "Jewish Community Rules," *The Laws of Palestine,* ed. by Robert Harry Drayton (London: Government of Palestine, 1934), III, 2132-2144.

36 The supreme judicial body in the Second Jewish State (third century B.C.—70 A.D.).

37 Hayim Greenberg [ed.], *Dath Israel u'Medinath-Israel* (New York: World Zionist Organization, 1950-1951), pp. 349-351.

38 "The Palestine Order in Council," *Constitutions, Laws, Treaties of States in the Near and Middle East,* ed. by Helen Miller Davis (Durham, N. C.: Duke University Press, 1953), pp. 349-351.

39 *Ibid.,* p. 352.

40 "Proclamation" [of the Provisional Council of the State of Israel], *Iton Rishmi* (Israel), May 14, 1948, p. 3.

41 "Jewish Community Rules," *The Laws of Palestine,* ed. by Robert Harry Drayton (London: Government of Palestine, 1939), III, 2132.

42 "Proclamation" [of the Provisional Council of the State of Israel], *Iton Rishmi* (Israel), May 14, 1948, p. 3.

43 *Sefer ha'Hukim* [Book of Laws], No. 133 (September 4, 1953), p. 165.

44 *State of Israel Government Yearbook* (Jerusalem: Government Printer, 1951-1952), p. 17.

45 Theodor Meron, "The Authority of Religion in Israel," *Jewish Frontier,* XXII (January, 1955), p. 22.

46 A Jewish ceremony which releases a widow and her brother-in-law from the duty of uniting in a levirate marriage. Talmud Bavli, Vol. Yebamot, 2A.

Part II

RELIGION IN THE NEW STATE OF ISRAEL

1. *Religion Vis-à-vis the State*

The State of Israel was created by the November 29, 1947 Resolution of the United Nations General Assembly[1] and by the Declaration of Independence issued by Israel's Provisional Council of State.[2] According to the first:

> Independent Arab and Jewish States and the Special International Regime for the City of Jerusalem, set forth in this Plan, shall come into existence in Palestine two months after the evacuation of the armed forces of the Mandatory Power has been completed, but, in any case, no later than October 1, 1948. . . . [1]

The same Resolution made it mandatory for the two newly created States to issue a Declaration containing the following provision:

> No discrimination of any kind shall be made between the inhabitants on the ground of race, religion, language, or sex. . . . The family laws and personal status of the various minorities and their religious interests, including endowments, shall be respected . . . [2]

The Declaration of Independence stated that:

> The State of Israel will open for Jewish immigration and for the Ingathering of the Exiles; it will foster the development of the country for the benefit of all its inhabitants; it will be based on freedom, justice, and peace as envisaged by the Prophets of Israel; it will ensure complete equality of social and political rights to all its inhabitants *irrespective of religion, race or sex; it will guarantee freedom of religion, conscience, language, education and culture;* it will safeguard the *Holy Places of all religions;* and it will be faithful to the *principles of the Charter of the United Nations.*[3] (Emphasis ours.)

The State of Israel has no written constitution.[4] It is governed by the law of the former British Mandatory Power, which, in turn, accepted much of the Turkish law.[5] For the sake of continuity and stability the entire body of laws in force when the British departed in 1948 was retained. Unless specific action was taken by the Knesset to change a law, it remained in effect.[6] The new State will wait for more peaceful days to draft a constitution.

Recognition of the Jewish law by the British authorities was regarded as a victory over the Arabs. During the Mandate, all Jews, as Zionists, accepted the establishment of Rabbinical Courts.

According to that law, Jews can be united in marriage only by their respective clerical officials. The Chief Rabbi designates the Rabbis empowered to solemnize marriages and establishes the religious courts which pass on divorces and inheritance rights.[7]

The law makes no provision for civil marriage, thus inhibiting mixed marriages. It deprives the individual of a right he enjoys in other countries. Moreover, the law, as it presently operates, makes Jewish marriage possible through the ministry of an orthodox Rabbi only. The right to designate officiating rabbis, as pointed out, is in the hands of the Chief Rabbi. He, up to the present, has designated only orthodox rabbis. Marriage of a *kohen*[8] to a divorcee is also barred by the orthodox Rabbinical Courts.[9]

In the early days of the Israeli State, the Provisional Council of State and the first Knesset set up a committee on constitution and law, headed by Zerach Warhaftig of the religious Hapoel Hamizrahi Party,[10] but in view of the uncompromising position of the religious parties, the Coalition Government decided to forego a new Constitution *in toto* and build it law by law instead.[11] In compliance with this decision, the Knesset voted on June 13, 1950 to adopt a constitution by evolution.[12] The laws passed since manifest great understanding of tradition by the secularists, despite the fact that a spirit of understanding does not always satisfy the religious parties. Though three new laws were passed in 1953—the State Education Law, the National Service Law, and the Rabbinical Courts Jurisdiction (Marriage and Divorce) Law—many more were held over from the days of the Mandate. A cursory examination of these laws might lead one to believe that Israel is a clerical state.

Not all the religious laws are unacceptable to the secularists. The progressive labor movement realizes, for instance, that the Sabbath should be the day of rest, sanctioned as it is by the traditions of thousands of years. That some consider it a religious ritual as well is not important. What interests the Israeli secularist is the social character of the day. Granted that observation of the Sabbath affects Government services. But this holds true of other countries, too, where on the official day of rest no mail is delivered. Why, then, say the secularists, shouldn't Israel accept it? The latter have therefore made great compromises in the matter of public transportation on the Sabbath, since travel on that day is rigorously fought by the religious authorities. In fact, though statistics indicate that 85 per cent of the population of Israel is not religious, there are not many instances of callous indifference to the sensibilities of religious Jews. Many districts in Jerusalem, or cities like B'nei Brak, close off all streets on the Sabbath by municipal ordinance and transportation on that day is strictly forbidden.

The State Education Law is the most revolutionary legislation passed in 1953 and is fundamentally altering the whole basis of education in Israel.[13] It sets up only two types of educational institutions—State Schools and State Religious Schools—though it grants official recognition to schools not under state administration. The implications of this new set-up can best be appreciated when it is recalled that in the 1952-53 school year there were 1600 schools under the control of the Histradruth[14] (including those affiliated to its Oved Dathi[15]); 593 controlled by the General Zionists-Progressives; 565 under the jurisdiction of the Mizrahi-Hapoel Hamizrahi group; 264 controlled by the Agudat Israel; and 135 which claimed to be independent.

The new law defines its purpose as follows: "To base fundamental [elementary] education in the state" (only elementary schools are covered by the law) "on values of the heritage of Israel and the achievements of science, on love for the country and fealty to the State of Israel and the Jewish people, on training in agriculture and manual labor, on pioneering, and on striving towards the creation of a society built on freedom, equality, tolerance, mutual help and love of mankind." [16]

It provides for the formulation of a standard curriculum obligatory in all State schools, comprising 75 percent of their program of studies, and of alternative supplementary programs, comprising 25 percent of the curriculum, to meet the wishes of parents. Two Advisory Councils—one for State Education, the other for State Religious Education—administer the Law. Where two-thirds of the parents of the children attending a school so desire, they can petition for the status of "recognized school." "Recognized schools" enjoy considerable autonomy. Though their curriculum must be approved by the Ministry of Education, they have the authority to engage and dismiss teachers and are granted a substantial annual subvention. Some schools previously in the Agudat Israel "trend" have taken advantage of this leeway and have formed a separate school network, involving some 17,000 pupils in 1954-55.[17] But Mapam (Israel's extreme left-wing party), which within the general framework of the Histradruth School Grouping controlled (and still controls) the schools in its own settlements, openly threatened to turn the law into a "scrap of paper."

The main feature of the Law is the abolition of the "trend" system which has prevailed in Israel's Jewish education for over thirty years. During the Mandatory period, the Jewish educational system was primarily the responsibility of the parents and was financed by voluntary contribution from the Jewish population under the general supervision of the Jewish Agency[18] and the Jewish National Council (Va'ad Leumi), with little support from the Mandatory Government. Because of this individual and community initiative, it was natural that the parents and organized bodies in the community should have sought to establish schools according to their respective ideologies or religiosity. Each group of such schools, largely autonomous in finance, administration, and educational philosophy, was known as a "trend." General opinion today favors the educational reforms instituted by the Government. It believes that the new Law is destined to be a landmark in the development of education and culture in Israel.

In September, 1949, the Knesset adopted the Defence Service Law,[19] which made women, as well as men, subject to the national service draft. It exempted mothers and pregnant women and specified that married women be called for reserve duty only. The Religious Bloc opposed the Law on the contention that army life is morally damaging to young women. The Government agreed, therefore, to exempt orthodox women if they testified to the sincerity of their religiosity. But, because of the cry of discrimination raised by non-orthodox women, it added two amendments. The first made it obligatory for orthodox women to prove their orthodoxy.[20] The second stipulated that religious women who refused to serve in the army be assigned either to agricultural tasks in a religious settlement or to social welfare work.[21]

Because of great pressure by the religious groups, the second amendment has not yet been put into effect.

The Rabbinical Courts Jurisdiction (Marriage and Divorce) Law,[22] even more than the compromises of the National Service Law, constitutes a signal victory for the Religious Bloc.

This law gives complete and exclusive control of all marriages and divorces in the Jewish community of Israel to the orthodox Rabbinical Courts. They are to rule on all cases brought before them according to the Law of the Torah.[23] Most important is the clause giving teeth to their edicts on marriage, divorce, and *halitsa*. Non-compliance with an order of the Rabbinical Court can be penalized by imprisonment. These enforcement provisions guarantee women full protection. And by safeguarding its religious basis, the law forestalls a division of the Jewish community into two camps whose children would be prevented from mingling in marriage by two equally valid marriage procedures—one religious, the other civil.[24]

Objectors to the Law contend that Israel needs a wall which would clearly separate Religion and State, so that exclusive authority over marriage and divorce does not rest in the hands of the orthodox Rabbinate. Not only should non-orthodox Rabbis have the right to officiate in accordance with *their* concepts of Judaism, but the men and women of Israel should, if they so desire, be enabled to seek marriage or divorce without religious authorization and to resort to civil authority for such sanctions. Religion is healthier in free hands than in societies where it has about it the elements of compulsion.

Some Jewish religious leaders, especially in the United States, admit that many orthodox religious laws, frozen for centuries, are not relevant to the conditions of our contemporary world. Israel's most serious problem, they say, is that too many people are indifferent to religion only because they have no alternative to an orthodox faith. Israel needs a modern progressive movement within Judaism, because at present even the religious Bar-Ilan University of the Mizrahi is too progressive for the ultra-orthodox religious groups.

At the rise of the State there were some 650,000 Jews in Israel; as of December 31, 1957 there were 1,762,741.[25] It is no mean task to find a common denominator for the German immigrant of the pre-Hitler era, brought up in the culture of Goethe and Schiller, and the Yemenite of a backward civilization. To weld these disparate elements together, one must, in addition to establishing a common language and common customs, seek out that which is binding and common to all, rather than what is distinctive: a uniform school system, a uniform army, and a uniform body of laws can do much to bring about unity. On the whole, there is today a spirit of tolerance towards religion, even on the part of the most extreme left-wing groups. There is sympathy for the religious drive, and the national, the social, and the positive are stressed in every religious ritual. Such is the secularist attitude. But the Religious Bloc is not ready for compromise. Its attitude was expressed by Dr. Itzhaak Herzog, Ashkenazi Chief Rabbi of Israel:

> The aim of Orthodox Jewry in Israel is to bring about a state law which will make the law of the Torah binding. It must be pointed out that even at present one of the basic laws of the State must be the observation of the Sabbath and Kashrut.[26] And we hope that with God's help the law of our Jewish State will be based on the tenets of the Torah.[27]

Such is the general stand of the religious group that, divided though it be into many parties—Neturei Karta, Agudat Israel, Poalei Agudat Israel, Hapoel Hamizrahi-Mizrahi, Haoved Hadati, which are, in turn, split into many subdivisions—has reconciled itself to the existence of the State.[28]

From the religious point of view, the Rabbinical Courts Jurisdiction Law is basic. It recognizes the exclusive jurisdiction of the Rabbinical Courts in all matters pertaining to marriage, divorce, alimony, and maintenance of children which affect Jews in the State of Israel. The Rabbinical Courts may order a husband to divorce his wife, a wife to accept a divorce, and a brother-in-law to give *halitsa* to a widow. Since, however, the jurisdiction of these Courts is restricted to matters of personal status, in the event of refusal by any of the parties involved to comply with a Rabbinical Court ruling the District Court is empowered, on the application of the Attorney General, to enforce the ruling by imprisonment.

Considering the strong views held on this subject and the body of influential opinion pressing for the institution of civil marriage, it is noteworthy that the Law was opposed in the Knesset only by the extreme left-wing parties. The spirit of this law can best be understood from some of its provisions:

1. Matters of marriage and divorce of Jews in Israel, whether nationals or residents of the State, shall be under the exclusive jurisdiction of Rabbinical Courts.

2. Marriages and divorces of Jews shall be performed in Israel in accordance with Jewish religious law.
3. Where a suit for divorce between Jews has been filed in a Rabbinical Court, whether by the wife or by the husband, a Rabbinical Court shall have exclusive jurisdiction in any matter connected with such suit, including maintenance for the wife and for the children of the couple.[29]

That this law stems from orthodox Jewry's uncompromising demands is evident from the following statement by Chief Rabbi Herzog:

> The cardinal thing is that marriage and divorce should be regulated by the law of the Jewish religion. . . . Provisions for an optional choice between religious and civil marriage or religious and civil court would imply a serious blow to the fundamental tenets of the Jewish religion and to family life. . . . This may eventually bring about a racial split between orthodox and non-orthodox Jewry and prevent intermarriage between them. . . .[30]

2. *The Ministry of Religious Affairs*

Non-religious circles in Israel contend that religion is a private affair and needs no intervention by the State. While ultra-orthodox Jews are critical of the fact that the Ministry of Religious Affairs includes departments concerned with non-Jewish religious problems.[31]

But it is necessary to provide for the religious organizational needs of each community, while, at the same time, coordinating the diverse practices and institutions of new immigrants from different countries. Special problems are also created by the fact that Israel is the holy cradle of other world religions—Christianity and Mohammedanism. There is, therefore, a need for coordinating relations between religion and State by a special State instrument. The Ministry of Religious Affairs is such an instrument.

The Ministry comprises the following Departments:

Jewish Religious Affairs
Rabbinate and Rabbinical Courts
Religious Councils
Moslem and Druze Religious Affairs
Christian Communities

The Department for Jewish Religious Affairs is composed of six sections:

1. The Religious Culture Section—which is concerned with the revival of ancient customs and traditions and their adaptation to the life of today.
2. The Holy Places Section—which seeks to maintain the dignity of the holy sites and historical monuments.
3. The Contact with the Diaspora Section—which seeks to strengthen the religious bonds between Israel and world Jewry.
4. The Public Services Section—which supervises Kashrut in the army, hospitals, and meat imports.
5. The Immigrant Settlement Section—which organizes the religious life in new settlements.
6. The Religious Institutions Section—which is concerned with the inspection of Yeshivoth.[32]

The Department of the Rabbinate and the Rabbinical Court deals with all administrative and financial matters relating to Rabbinical Courts. There are seventeen Rabbinical Courts of the First Instance and a Rabbinical Court of Appeal in Jerusalem. The Department also pays the rabbis' salaries, takes care of their administrative needs, providing them with supplies, and has charge of the registration of marriages and divorces.

The Religious Councils Department deals with the maintenance of religious activities in Israel's communities, coordinates and supervises all such activities.

The Moslem and Druze Department supervises the religious education and social welfare of the Moslems and pays the salaries of their religious personnel and courts.

Israel's Christian citizens are divided into three religious groups—Catholic, Greek Orthodox, and Protestant. The work of the Department of Christian Communities is based on the principle of absolute non-intervention in the internal affairs of these groups. Its most important task is the safeguarding of the Christian holy sites.[33]

3. *The Rabbinate*

In March, 1921, the British High Commissioner of Palestine convoked a gathering of Jewish community leaders and rabbis in office to vote on Jewish religious institutions. The delegates voted for the rabbis in office, and the Government later officially approved this as the Rabbinical Council.

The Rabbinical Council is composed of two Chief Rabbis and six Associate Rabbis. It is Israel's religious authority and exercises supervision over local rabbinical offices, which sit as Rabbinical Courts of the First Instance. The Rabbinical Council itself serves as a Court of Appeal in matters over which the Rabbinical Courts have jurisdiction.[34]

As empowered by the Palestine Order in Council, the Rabbinical Courts have:

1. Exclusive jurisdiction in matters of marriage and divorce, alimony, and confirmation of wills of members of their community other than foreigners.

2. Jurisdiction in any other matter of personal status of such persons where all the parties to the action consent to their jurisdiction.

3. Exclusive jurisdiction over any case pertaining to the constitution or internal administration of a Wakf[35] or religious endowment established before the Rabbinical Court according to Jewish Law.[36]

And according to an Ordinance providing for the organization of religious communities, we find in the "Jewish Community Rules" of the Knesset Israel the following:

> The Rabbinical Council shall be the recognized religious representative of the community in relation to the Government of Palestine; and the local Rabbi or Rabbinical Office shall be the recognized religious representative of the local community in relation to the district administration.[37]

The regulations governing the election of the Rabbinical Council, Rabbinical Offices, and Rabbis of local communities provide that:

> An Electoral Committee for the election of the Rabbinical Council shall nominate forty-two Rabbis from a list of officiating Rabbis in Palestine submitted by the Rabbinical Council and twenty-eight laymen from a list submitted by the General Council (Va'ad Leumi)[38] to the Electoral Assembly for the election of the Rabbinical Council.[38]

Each list of candidates is to "contain the names of not more than eight candidates, of whom four shall be Sephardic[39] and four Ashkenazic. . . .[40] The nominators shall mark 'Chief Rabbi' against the names of two candidates for the offices of 'Chief Rabbi,' one of whom shall be a Sephardic, and the other an Ashkenazi Rabbi . . ."[41]

The same regulations also prescribe the term of office:

> The term of office of the Rabbinical Council shall be five years as from the date of its election.[42]

For the election of Rabbis of local communities, the law provides that, "the Rabbinical Office or the Rabbi of any local community shall be elected by a Special Assembly consisting of the members of the Committee of the local community concerned and representatives of the large local synagogues to be selected jointly by the local Rabbinical Council and the Committee of the local community whose number shall be equal to that of the members of the Committee of the local community." [43]

The power of the Chief Rabbis is outlined in the following provision: "The election of Rabbinical Offices and of Rabbis of local communities shall be subject to the approval of the Rabbinical Council." [44]

Upon the death of Chief Rabbi Abraham Itzhak Kook (1865-1935), the Electoral Assembly chose, in accordance with the law outlined above, two Chief Rabbis—the Ashkenazi Rabbi, Dr. Itzhak Halevy Herzog, and the Sephardic Rabbi, Yaakov Meir (1856-1939)—and six members of the Rabbinical Council. When Chief Rabbi Meir died in 1939, the Assembly replaced him by his first deputy, Rabbi Benzion Hai Uziel.[45] At Rabbi Uziel's death, Rabbi Itzhak Nissim was elected Chief Sephardic Rabbi.

When Israel became an independent State, the Provisional Council of State, on May 14, 1948, issued the following proclamation:

> So long as no laws have been enacted on behalf of the Provisional Council of State, the law which existed in Palestine on the 5th year 5078 [May 14, 1948] shall continue in force in the State of Israel.[46]

The election over, the Rabbinical Council made the following administrative arrangements at its inaugural meeting:

1. The Rabbinical Council will, under the Presidium of the two Chief Rabbis, be the Court of Appeals.

2. The Rabbinical Council will supervise all Rabbinical Offices in the country as well as the rabbis in each local community.

3. All Rabbinical Courts must be approved by the Rabbinical Council.

4. The Rabbinical Council will appoint special rabbis to officiate at marriages and divorces in settlements too small for a permanent rabbi.[47]

To date (March, 1959) this Rabbinical Council Law is still in effect.

With the exception of the extremist Neturei Karta, orthodox Jewry in Israel, with the Rabbinate as its spokesman, has followed a pragmatic policy towards the State. In 1952 Dr. Joseph Burg, former Israeli Minister of Posts and Hapoel Hamizrahi leader, stated:

> The religious Zionist Parties decided that religious Jews cannot isolate themselves from the normal processes of the Jewish State. By being part of the government they can strengthen religious Judaism in Israel. This has been demonstrated time and again during the last year. This was the reason for joining the formation of the government after consultation with the Chief Rabbinate.
>
> Hapoel Hamizrahi and Mizrahi recognize the Chief Rabbinate as the final authority on all religious questions. They think that it is unthinkable that certain circles should rely on the opinion of rabbis of their own choice for their action. In the Jewish State the central Torah authority is the Chief Rabbinate—which is elected by the entire Jewish community.[48]

A similar attitude of compromise with the State is reflected in the Rabbinate's approach to the controversial National Service Law. At the First American National Conference of Religious Jewry for Israel held in New York, April 4, 1954, Chief Rabbi Itzhak Halevy Herzog delivered the following message:

> We are exerting our best efforts in respect to the problems of National Service for Women in Israel, and there is an excellent prospect that the issues will be resolved through achievement of an understanding with the Government of Israel to the satisfaction of all concerned. . . .
>
> The attitude of the Chief Rabbinate of Israel, which has been transmitted to you previously, is that WE HAVE NOT PROHIBITED NATIONAL SERVICE FOR WOMEN ON THE BASIS OF OUR HOLY LAW. We simply transmitted to the Knesset and the leaders of our society a request that this bill be removed from

> the agenda because of doubts, in certain cases, concerning necessary protection of feminine modesty. Then we became convinced that this proposed law had a sure majority in the Knesset, even without the votes of the religious representatives. The government also assured us that the law would be implemented with respect for our religious and ethical principles, that in such implementation the feelings of all religious circles would be taken into consideration, and especially that certain categories of girls from such circles would be exempted entirely from national service. . . . [49]

What is the attitude of the two Chief Rabbis to actual religious problems?

In matters involving property disputes and civil suits, Chief Rabbi Herzog is willing to employ the stratagems of Jewish law in order to conform to the requirements of democratic thought. He would not disqualify a woman from serving as a witness in court. Though in matters of marriage and divorce he insists on the exclusive jurisdiction of the Rabbinate, he holds that divorce laws should be regulated to protect the rights of women. He offers it as a general principle that "the Jewish State, in the framework of the Torah and with due regard for reality, will be necessarily neither entirely theocratic nor entirely democratic." [50]

The second Chief Rabbi, the late Benzion Uziel, was eager to re-establish the ancient system of rabbinic jurisprudence in its fullness, deferring little, if at all, to the realities of modern Jewish life. "The hour sets the demand and obligation upon us of renewing the building and the establishment of High Courts in Jerusalem, from which place it will in time be removed to its chosen place, the Hall of Hewn Stones in the Holy Temple in Jerusalem." [51]

There is some conflict between orthodox and reform Jewry, with the Rabbinate as the target. The less orthodox elements complain that the leaders of the more extreme Agudat Israel are trying to undermine the authority of the Chief Rabbinate by claiming that other religious leaders[52] possess that authority, and that such attacks on the Rabbinate undermine the whole basis of religious life is Israel. The Chief Rabbinate is recognized by the Israeli government as the official religious spokesman whose decisions are authoritative. To ignore it is, therefore, an act which no responsible religious Jew should accept, because such a step is a threat to the religious life of the State.[53]

That the power of the Rabbinate is a stumbling block in the path of religious modernization cannot be denied. Only the Chief Rabbi, for instance, can authorize a Rabbi to perform the marriage ceremony. A diploma from a recognized rabbinical school is not sufficient. "Religious modernism," said Ben-Zion Bokser, "is confronted with great difficulties. The power of the organized community is against it. A rabbi who conducts a service where the sexes would not be separated would lose his right to officiate at marriages. Even orthodox rabbis, if they dress in Western style and are clean shaven, would find it almost impossible to follow their calling in Israel." [54]

Other aspects of the Rabbinate's rule also call for criticism. The synagogue stands apart from the world. The rabbis are city or town employees and, attached to the Kehilla,[55] they busy themselves only with ritual matters. Neither the synagogues nor the Rabbinate as a whole have anything to do with youth work or education.

4. *Religion in Politics*

Israel is a multi-party state. The make-up and politics of these parties are revealed in the following self-definitions:[56]

MAPAI (Israel Labor Party)

> A Zionist Socialist Party aiming at the ingathering of the Jewish People, the upbuilding of the State of Israel, and a socialist regime founded on spiritual and political freedom. Its internal policy stands for democracy and a planned economy based on the development of the cooperative sector in coordination with the development of constructive public and private enterprise. . . .

HERUT MOVEMENT

A party founded by the Irgun Zvai Leumi in opposition to the present regime in Israel. It calls for the territorial integrity of Eretz Israel . . . within its historic boundaries on both sides of the Jordan, for private initiative in the economic and social structure of the State. . . .

GENERAL ZIONIST PARTY

The Party stands for free private enterprise, the establishment of Government health services and Government labour exchanges, the achievement of economic independence through increased attraction of investment, capital.

NATIONAL RELIGIOUS PARTY—HAPOEL HAMIZRAHI & MIZRAHI

The aims of the Party are: *the establishment of a society based on the ethical and social principles of Israel's Torah; the striving after legislation founded on the laws of the Torah . . . the preservation of the specifically "Jewish" or Torah character of the State in all branches of life. . . .* (Emphasis ours.)

ACHDUT HA'AVODA—POALEI ZION

A pioneering Zionist Socialist Party, standing for: ingathering of Jews of all countries in a Socialist Jewish State in the whole of Palestine by peaceful means; planned economy, widespread agricultural settlement, cooperation of Zionist Socialist Parties within Government. . . .

MAPAM (United Workers Party)

A left-wing Zionist Socialist Party, aiming at the ingathering of the Jewish People . . . the realization of socialism and the training of Jewish youth in Israel and the Diaspora for pioneering settlement. It stands for progressive social legislation, and opposes all discrimination within the State. . . . Its programme postulates a Labour Government in coalition with all progressive forces; an economy planned for the absorption of large-scale immigration; Jewish-Arab working class solidarity. . . .

AGUDAT ISRAEL PARTY

> *The Party stands for the strictest observance of the Torah in the administration of the State, with jurisdiction entrusted to rabbinical authorities. . . .* (Emphasis ours.)

POALEI AGUDAT ISRAEL (Agudat Israel Workers' Party)

> *No legal code other than that of the Torah is acceptable for the State of Israel. . . . The Party opposes the formal equality of men and women.*[57] (Emphasis ours.)

COMMUNIST PARTY OF ISRAEL

> Basing itself on Marxist-Leninist theory, it aims at socialism in Israel. . . .

PROGRESSIVE PARTY

> The Progressive Party is a non-socialist party with progressive liberal tendencies, comprising both middle and working class membership. . . . [58]

So great a multiplicity of parties calls for government tact and discretion. Political leaders must ever bear in mind that temporary compromises which are not decisive and which serve the needs of the people and the State are a political necessity.

A particularly stormy petrel is the extremist Neturei Karta group. It regards Israel as not a Jewish, but a Zionist State only. It has carried its ultra-religious stand to its *reductio ad absurdum* by refusing to serve in Israel's army, to carry identity cards, to use ration books, to avail itself of any government services, etc. The Government does not take the Neturei Karta too seriously, convinced that it is but a temporary phenomenon which will eventually disappear.

It is difficult to determine the exact number of religious Jews in Israel. In the 1955 elections, they sent seventeen representatives to a Knesset seating 120, indicating, apparently, that only some 14 percent of Israeli Jews are religious and the rest anti-religious. But these figures do not reflect the true picture. Only a small group of communists, with six seats in the Knesset and representing but 4½ percent of the voters, can be termed anti-religious. Even Mapam, representing with its nine seats in the Knesset less than 10 percent of the voters, cannot be defined as anti-religious, only as non-religious. And the two major parties, Mapai and the General Zionists—who together represent nearly 50 percent of the voters with fifty-three seats in the Knesset[59]—though also non-religious, have deep reverence for the traditions of the Torah and profound desire to avoid strife. Leaders in both these parties take into consideration national tradition, international opinion, Jewish public opinion in the United States, and the danger of a national schism. These leaders, with Premier David Ben-Gurion in the vanguard, gave up a Constitution already drafted because of religious opposition. This Constitution, drafted by Dr. Leo Kohn, political counsel to the Ministry of Foreign Affairs, carried the following provisions:

Preamble

To establish our State on the principles and visions of our prophets.[60]

Part II

No freedom of assembly or demonstration against religion. . . .[61]

Part III

State legislation is to be based largely on Hebrew law.[62]

Orthodox Jewry considered these provisions unsatisfactory. Rabbi Yitzhak Meir Levin, leader of Agudat Israel, voiced their basic demands at a Knesset session:

> Orthodox Jewry aspires to a law that is based on the law of the Torah, and only that law should dominate all aspects of life in the country. . . . I must stress that *legislation which is not grounded in the law of the Torah will be regarded by Orthodox Jewry as provisional law.*[63]

For an appraisal of the political problem created by religion in Israel, it is well to refer to the views of leading spokesmen for both the religious and the non-religious parties. According to the *Mizrahi Weg*,[64] organ of the moderately religious Mizrahi Party in the United States, five major problems plague the orthodox Jews.

1. The number of Jewish children being taken into the net of mission schools. The solution of this problem is entangled in complicated international law regarding minorities and religious freedom, which cannot be bypassed.[65]

2. The dearth of meat in Israel. Because non-kosher pig meat is not under control, many people have gone into hog raising. This has created difficulties, for it is against the law to prohibit the sale of ham or pork to Christians.

3. The question of education. The Government, as previously stated, has taken over all elementary education and has established two departments: the Department of Education and a special religious department. A Religious Council for Education has also been organized, with representatives from the following groups: The Rabbinate, Mizrahi and Poalei Mizrahi, Poalei Agudat Israel, "Religious Workers," and other impartial orthodox Jews, to see that a true religious spirit reigns in the schools.[66]

4. Observation of the Sabbath.[67] Though there are special Sabbath laws, permission to work on the Sabbath has been granted to transportation personnel and to certain vital industries. This problem has been debated in the Knesset and some solutions have been arrived at.

5. The National Service Law in its application to women.[68] Ways and means to guard the morality of orthodox girls, who are duty-bound to serve in the Government, have been introduced and adopted.

The circles responsible for the clamor about the National Service Law advance two reasons, which, in their opinion, make this problem such an important one: 1. That some great rabbis have banned national service for women; 2. That it is the first time that the Government has compelled a section of religious Jews to do something that, according to their convictions, is against the laws of the Torah.

It is important to realize that the edict of the rabbis was issued before the Service Law (for women) was adopted and that, at the time, there was no conception of what this Bill would mean, because the impression prevailed that it would call for recruitment of orthodox girls for military service. The Law, however, at the request of the Chief Rabbinate and of Mizrahi representatives, was greatly modified, so that it is altogether different from the one originally envisioned. The Mizrahi Party found nothing with which to quarrel and, consequently, voted for it. The *Mizrahi Weg* of January-February, 1954 defended this vote as follows:

> It is regrettable that the majority know nothing about this law. They are, for example, unaware that girls who had at one time been exempted from military service will not be called to National Service, which means that all religious girls . . . will be exempt from all and any service if their parents declare that they lead a strictly religious life. Nor do these Jews know that girls who get married during their National Service year will be demobilized.
>
> Girls in service will be given every opportunity to stay in religious surroundings or in their home towns, in which case they may sleep at home. . . .

To appease the religious groups of the government coalition, the Knesset passed the Rabbinical Courts Jurisdiction Law giving the Rabbinate complete jurisdiction over marriage and divorce.[69] The opposition to this Law claims that it is theocratic dictatorship, but the Chief Rabbinate asserts that where the creation of a unified state is at stake, it is, at times, necessary to use some forms of compulsion.[70]

The Sabbath demonstrations of the religious extremists, the Neturei Karta, in Jerusalem, and the fist fights in Meah She'arim, have provoked debates on the probability of a "culture battle" (Kulturkampf) in Israel. It is interesting to note that, despite the fact that the Neturei Karta does not recognize the

State of Israel and demands the internationalization of Jerusalem, its Sabbath demonstrations are supported by the Mizrahi movement which was part of the coalition Government as recently as July, 1958, as well as by the Agudat Israel, which, at one time, was also a member of the Government. In other words, a group of Jews hostile to the Government is supported by parties who are, or were, part of the coalition Government.

Allied against this united religious front is the whole non-orthodox community of Israel—both those who belong to the coalition and those who oppose it.

A "culture battle" would be a major catastrophe for the State of Israel. The orthodox groups realize the gravity of the situation as well as the unorthodox. The Israeli community is composed of dozens of different cultures which must be fused into one cultural unit. The carriers of the various cultures belong to many tribes with centuries-old traditions, and no tribe is ready to give up its traditional way of life.[71]

The Israeli Government has, however, embarked on a process of hastening the integration of the new citizens into the life and culture of the land. But it knows that progress will be slow. It does not agree with advocates of drastic measures. It knows that culture imposed by power is brutal and is not culture at all. Its policy is therefore a positive one. The community is urged to learn the new way of life without giving up old traditions. The hope and goal are gradual adoption of new cultural values and the discarding of outdated ones.

In the solution of religious problems, the Government is more careful still, for religion among Jews is more than just a faith. In the course of thousands of years of dispersion, religion has been the national symbol of Judaism. An irreligious Jew condemns apostasy almost as much as an orthodox Jew. Precisely because of such an attitude towards religion, the problem in Israel is manifold, and the ultra-orthodox factions take advantage of this circumstance to play power politics.

It may be that the secular community is more to be blamed for this unfortunate situation than the orthodox. For economic and political expediency, the first has, perhaps, made too many concessions to the religious elements. Said the *Forward* in December, 1954:

> When they deliberated on the emerging Jewish State, the middle-of-the road Jews realized clearly that it would be a modern country and that it would be necessary to adjust the laws of religion to those of the State. They foresaw a situation which would necessitate the convoking of a Sanhedrin[72] of Rabbis to find a way out from the various religious precepts that cannot be carried out in a modern country with a ramified economy. There are hundreds of activities in a modern country that must go on uninterruptedly, but which are forbidden by religious law to be pursued on the Sabbath. An orthodox Jew will not use the telephone on Saturday, knowing that a conversation by phone necessitates certain electric and mechanic functions which are forbidden on the Sabbath. Or, when he turns the faucet for a glass of water, he knows that the water is brought up by a machine driven by electricity which is being created then and there. However, some things which cannot be helped are overlooked by even pious, orthodox Jews.
>
> The Neturei Karta, however, consider a modern Jewish country—heresy . . . They believe that when the true Messiah comes and redeems the Jews, circumstances will be created which will make it possible to observe all the laws of the Torah and, at the same time, have an independent State with its multifarious services.
>
> But the middle-of-the-roaders did not wait for Messiah with his miraculous organization. They endeavored earnestly to find a way out. Fortunately for them, they did not need to instigate reforms. The Government granted them more religious concessions than they themselves expected. They were spared the necessity of convoking a Sanhedrin to inaugurate reforms. The irreligious Government party assumed the role of Sanhedrin. Its concessions, however, played into the hands not only of the Mizrahi, but of the Agudat Israel, who envisioned an opportunity to gain more than political and economic concessions. They would gain religious power over the Government.

So the religious groups and the majority party—Mapai—made a coalition. The religious parties were not to meddle in the political and economic affairs in which Mapai was most interested in return for a free hand in all religious affairs. But when the religious parties realized that Mapai could not dominate the Government without their support, they began to demand more and more power. That is why there were so many crises in the coalition, and why Mapai invariably conceded. As a result, the orthodox factions of Israel, though comprising only 12% of the state, dominate the civic life of the whole community from cradle to grave. The entire family life is controlled by the Rabbis. They have more rights in that life than the Government. The Government has practically no say in the matter of marriage or divorce.[73] The Rabbinic Court has the same rights as the State Court, and the Rabbinic judges are paid by the Government.

As a result of these wholesale concessions, Mapai was compelled, because of political and economic pressures, to withdraw some of its regulations, while those conceded to the religious Bloc remained intact.

In time, Mapai realized that the successive concessions to the religious elements were leading dangerously close to a theocratic form of government. To prevent such an eventuality, it formed a coalition with the General Zionists. The Mizrahi, however, remained in the Government, hoping for a split in the coalition, in which case Mapai would again need them and, perhaps, even the Agudat Israel. In such an eventuality, the religious bloc would again be in a position to bargain with Mapai in the matter of religious laws. But to this day the hoped for split has not occurred. Difficult as it is, the coalition with the General Zionists is still in force, and the hopes of the religious parties for further concessions have not materialized.[74] At the present time the religious parties are looking for ways and means to reacquire their former never-to-be-forgotten concessions. Such ways and means came their way through the Neturei Karta. It is therefore understandable that the religious parties, both those who are in coalition with Mapai and those who were formerly members of it, should defend the actions of the Neturei Karta.

> The Neturei Karta are understood and tolerated by tolerant people; they are truly pious. Their piety is their greatest possession, nothing else is of any consequence in their life. They await Messiah and are hostile to those who doubt his eventual appearance. They live a secluded, ultra-orthodox life in Meah She'arim, and no one interferes with their way of life. But *they* want to turn all Jerusalem into a great Meah She'arim.[75]

A cooperative point of view towards the "religion-vs.-the-state" problem was also expressed by Moshe Shapira, former Minister of Religious Affairs in Israel, in his address at the National Conference of Religious Jewry for Israel, held April 4, 1954 in New York:

> We cannot overlook the fact that in Israel there are two diametrically opposed *Weltanschauungen:* the religious one and the anti-religious one. The problem is where to find the Golden Mean, so that both will be able to live and build Israel. . . . Not by war and force will we bring back the non-religionists, but rather through our influence and by showing that the Jewish people cannot exist without the Torah. . . . Israel without Torah life and without the "mussur" [76] of her prophets is another Lebanon or Syria. . . .
>
> Since the establishment of the state, we have stood by the following principles:
>
> The unity and completeness of the Rabbinical Courts and the observance of Torah laws concerning marriage and divorce.
>
> The unity of the religious educational system.
>
> *Status quo* on Shabbat and Kashrut.
>
> These three basic foundations, according to our belief and the belief of the Chief Rabbinate, are the expressions of the categorical imperative for Jewish governmental life. . . .
>
> When the religious Marriage and Divorce Law was accepted by the Knesset, the Chief Rabbi declared at an assembly of *Dayanim*[77] that the day of the law is instituted ought to be considered a holiday for religious world Jewry. . . . The *Dayan* has equal status with the judge, both have the same rights, and the prestige of the *Dayan* has been upheld in Israel.[78]

Hapoel Hamizrahi claims that from its inception its policy towards the vexing question has been:

> Stay in the Zionist movement. Its Zionism was not a passive but a positive, constructive one. Our *Chaverim*[79] drained swamps, cleared fields, built roads, *Kibbutzim*,[80] *Moshavot*,[81] participated in defense and all constructive activities under more strenuous and unfavorable circumstances, enduring even greater hardships than other *Chalutzim*.[82] At the present, H. H. [Hapoel Hamizrahi] cooperates with the Government and all parties and forces in the upbuilding of *Eretz Israel*,[83] even though sinners they be.
>
> We firmly believe that the establishment of *Medinat Israel*[83] and the circumstances accompanying this event is an *Aschalta D'Geula*, the beginnings of a true redemption. Miracles do not occur in vain.
>
> In the economic upbuilding of Eretz Israel, progress must be made gradually, "little by little." Let no one seek a complete Paradise all at once. The same approach must be followed in the religious spiritual fields. We aim at the realization of the full Torah program, but step by step, "little by little."
>
> We recognize the properly constituted authority of the Chief Rabbinate for all religious problems in Israel, including the question of "Civilian Service for Women."
>
> We shall try to convince the American religious Jews to recognize that ours is the right path and that deeds, helping a religious Kibbutz or a Moshav or even purchasing an Israel bond, are more effective for a Torah true life in Israel than many protest parades and eloquent protest speeches.[84]

A clear analysis of the two major approaches—orthodox and secular—to the religious issue was given in the Israeli newspaper the *Palestine Post* (now the *Jerusalem Post*):

> It is true [Dr. A. Barth said] that even Jewish religion and tradition in their completeness no longer exist for the majority of the Jewish people, but part by part, precept by precept, trend by trend, they are to be found among the greater part.

And it is when those forms of life for the Jewish people in its Homeland are established on traditional lines that there will be created that widest possible common background . . .

The Jewish religion and tradition is the only thing that unites us. What else will be common to the immigrant from America and the immigrant from the Yemen, the newcomer from England and the one from Iraq, the Jew from Romania and the Jew from Morocco, if we do not create for them such forms of life as will recall for the majority common associations, and in particular those associations belonging to the common past of the people? And just in this our people is richly endowed. For the connection between the religious life and Jewish history is so close that when we base our policies on the Jewish religion, we thereby greatly strengthen most of the connections between the past and the future. . . .

Every injunction among the laws of Israel is one of the stones which altogether make up the house in which the People of Israel will re-discover its unity.

Let us not accept the superficial view which claims that the preservation of tradition in the Diaspora[85] was necessary as a bulwark against assimilation, a danger which does not exist in this country. We have no desire to cast away what we have learned, and we shall continue to learn, from the cultures of other peoples, but accept the blessing "God will enlarge Japhet, and He will dwell in the tenets of Shem." [86] To this end, however, we must strive that our tenets be the tenets of Shem. In other words, unless we set up the structure of our State under a leadership giving us and those who follow us the fundamental Jewish precepts, we are heading for Levantinism and are far from independent culture.[87]

Salomon Ginzberg, a secularist, rebutted the above arguments:

Dr. Barth's assumption that the religious way of life alone unites scattered Jewry is a matter of fact not correct.

It is to be noted that the religious link he wants us to build upon is not a vague allegiance to the principles and institutions of Judaism, some of which may indeed be worth taking over;

nor is it the lukewarm observance exemplified by attending synagogue on Yom Kippur[88] or abstaining from bacon. What he demands is the undiluted observance of the Law, complete with its 613 commandments and prohibitions,[89] including the injunction, specifically mentioned by him, not to wear a garment made of linen and wool. Such hundred-per-cent orthodoxy does not seem to prevail among the younger Jews even of Iraq or Morocco, and certainly not of Poland or Romania, let alone of America or Western Europe. The split in Jewry on the issue of orthodox observance did not originate with the Yishuv,[90] nor is it confined to it. . . . The common denominator of Jewish religion is just as frail in the Diaspora as it is here, and any national unity that could be built thereon would be about as substantial as the brotherhood in God between Rabbi Stephen Wise[91] and Rabbi Blau Amram.[92] [93]

"Why do you mix religion with politics? Religion is a personal matter, and you have no right to introduce it into politics and thereby confuse issues." Such is the question often addressed to the religious elements of Israel.

The late Zvi Perez Chajes,[94] noted Chief Rabbi of Vienna, answered it:

Is there any aspect of our economic, social, or spiritual life which cannot be classed as political? Even our religious life is bound up with our communal institutions and activities. The freedom for religious activities as well as the freedom of thought was achieved after a political struggle. There is no feature of our communal organization which is not connected, in one way or another, with politics, and this should not detract from the value of our activities. The political song only sounds unpleasant when sung by those who have no ear for political music. If one takes part in politics with clean hands, then politics is not a "dirty business." There is nothing which cannot be defiled, just as there is nothing which cannot be sanctified.[95]

5. *Religion-vs.-State Conflict*

An accurate definition of the term "religious" as it is applied in Israel is almost impossible. It is just as impossible to present statistics on the number of religious Jews in Israel.

Shortly after the establishment of the State, the Ministry of Religious Affairs published figures, based on the registration for the rationing system, which showed that over 80 percent of the Jews in Israel preferred kosher meat. But many people not necessarily religious do not eat *trefa* (non-kosher) meat because of tradition.

Neither does the existence of religious parties solve the statistical problem. Some religious Jews, being economic pragmatists, vote for the secular parties and are members of the Histadrut. The 14 percent which voted for the religious parties[96] can hardly be accepted as a true estimate of the situation.

If going once a year to the synagogue is a criterion of being religious (and this is indeed a sweeping definition), then 20 percent of the population falls within this category.[97]

The dominant groups in Israel are generally secular. They represent the labor movement and the pioneering elements. The Zionism of the pioneers was a revolutionary movement, and the culture they created was a secular one. Left-wing Mapam is in opposition to religion. Under its influence, the Declaration of the Establishment of the State of Israel omitted all reference to God.[98]

With the population thus divided into two camps, conflicts between religion and the state are inevitable.

While the ultra-orthodox Agudat Israel Party was part of the Government coalition, a flimsy peace reigned. But not for long.[99] When the fundamental issue of the character the State should assume arose, the conflict between religious and secular parties reached major proportions. The non-religious representatives envisioned a modern secular state with a modern constitution, but the religious leaders favored a more theocratic state. One thing led to another. First there was the question of the recruitment of women for national service, then the marriage and divorce laws. These were followed by the problem of the *Dayanim,* religious judges, which was the subject of violent debate in the Knesset. The issue at stake was the sole jurisdiction of religious judges in all matters pertaining to family life. Here it became apparent that there is a vast difference between the thinking of the general population and that of the religious minority.[100]

To be sure, neither of the two opposing forces is interested in keeping the conflict alive. The non-religious leaders showed understanding in realizing that in a Jewish state, religion and religious traditions must play a far from negligible role. They therefore made concessions in many areas: in the problem of Sabbath rest, the import of non-kosher meat, military service for religious girls. The religious leaders, too, want a peaceful solution. They promised loyalty to the Government. But no sooner did the primary question of the character of the Jewish State arise, that is, the type of Judaism the State should promote, than a deep rift developed between the two camps.

The representatives of the religious Jews openly admit that they do not feel bound by the laws of the Knesset, only by the laws given to the Jews by God on Mt. Sinai. They will therefore always follow the laws of God against those made by man.[101]

When the *Dayanim* law granting religious judges sole jurisdiction over family life was being debated in the Knesset, they promised to swear allegiance to the State, *but not to the State laws.* This aroused the ire of the entire Knesset. Knesset members of all secular parties—conservative, liberal, and leftist—joined in a united front against the *Dayanim* law, proclaiming that the *Dayanim* were not equipped to sit in judgment on matters of family life in a modern state.[102]

After the first (1949), the second (1951), and third (1955) elections, Mapai emerged as the largest party, but it did not command a majority in the Knesset.[103] It was necessary, therefore, to establish a coalition government. Left-wing Mapam demanded too big a price for its participation in a coalition. (After the 1955 election Mapam did join in a coalition.) The only other force was the religious Bloc,[104] and a coalition was established between it and Mapai. It enabled the Bloc to successfully press many of its religious demands.[105]

These demands of the Bloc and its readiness to force a government crisis present Israel with a serious problem. There can, it is true, be no question about the outcome of a *Kulturkampf*. The majority of Israel's population would not long tolerate dictation in matters affecting their private lives. But, though the outcome of a *Kulturkampf* is not in doubt, it would still be best to avoid it.

Later, Mapai tried to minimize the power of the religious parties through a coalition with the General Zionists in the hope of creating a two-party system in the future.[106] This attempt failed and the coalition dissolved after the 1955 election.

A problem arose with the creation of the Israeli Army—the problem of *Kashrut*. Responsible authorities decided that there was no room for both kosher and non-kosher kitchens in that army. The Jewish soldier had suffered many privations in European armies for lack of kosher food. How then could his own State, for which he and his fathers had struggled for centuries, refuse to provide him with it? Besides, *Kashrut* is a question of conscience. The religious soldier is prohibited from eating non-kosher food, but the non-religious soldier can eat kosher food without any damage to his sensitivity. For the sake of unity, it was decided therefore to burden the budget and provide the army with kosher food.[107] It was realized that in a mature society compromises must be made. Israel is a democratic State. In a matter of conscience the majority does not force its will on the minority.

In the First World War, many West-European countries allowed proven pacifists to serve as first-aid workers or completely absolved them from military service. In Israel, a great debate raged in connection with the conscription of women. Here a question of security was at stake. The secular parties felt that the religious Bloc was trying to take political advantage of the situation. The Defence Service Law of 1949[108] included women from 18 to 26 in the draft, except those who claimed exemption on religious grounds. Surprisingly, the women of the religious Hapoel Hamizrahi Party did not claim exemption, whereas many non-religious women took advantage of the exemption proviso.

In 1953, great consideration was given to bills of particular importance to the orthodox section of the community. This is the more notable because at the time the two major parties (Mapai and the General Zionists) in the coalition had a secure majority without the votes of their religious coalition partners, and these measures encountered strong opposition within the ranks of both Mapai and the General Zionists.

The most controversial measure of the year was the National Service Law.[109] The passage of this law was marked by unprecedented public demonstration of opposition. The object of the Bill was to provide alternative forms of national service for young women who, under the Defence Service Law, were subject to twenty-four months army service, but who objected to military duty on conscientious or religious grounds. These alternative services are: work in a religious agricultural settlement or institution, work in an Israeli Army office, work in an immigrant camp, and work in a social-welfare, educational, medical, or some other socially desirable institution to be determined *not by the Minister of Defense but by the Minister of Labor.*

There were two major concessions to religious opinion in the Bill: placing its administration under the authority of the Ministry of Labor and granting explicit permission to religious girls to sleep in their own homes, if they could so manage, and not in army barracks.

The strength of the ultra-orthodox opposition to the Bill surprised its sponsors, and especially the more moderate religious parties, who had accepted it as a reasonable compromise between religious objections to the conscription of women and military service. The controversy provoked public debate on the utility, from a military point of view, of conscripting young women for service in the army and of the advisability of compelling them to live in army barracks.

Despite these intermittent flare-ups, the secularists' earlier antagonistic attitude towards religion is no longer a fact in Israel. Respect and esteem for traditional Judaism have replaced that attitude.

But the political situation finds the religious groups unable to reach an agreement among themselves. Differing points of view separate them. There is no unity. Religious parties disagree on technical points, and it is possible for one party to be in the Government and the rest in the Opposition,[110] for some of them to support education under government supervision and others to insist on their own independent educational system.[111]

The Neturei Karta refuses to recognize either the State or Government of Israel, and conducts a *mitzvah*[112] campaign against them. The Chief Rabbinate is divided into two sections, Ashkenazi and Sephardic. In addition, the Agudat Israel has established its own rabbinate, and the Neturei Karta *its* own Chief Rabbi.

There are still other religious authorities: Dr. Isaiah Leibowitz, spiritual head of Haoved ha-Dati (religious workingmen), and Rabbi Shlomo Goren, chief military chaplain. These rabbis maintain that Jewish oral law[113] is primarily a visionary one that developed in anticipation of an ideal future state. The strict application of this law would, according to them, precipitate a crisis in the young state, where the majority of the population is non-orthodox. Conversely, the orthodox elements strongly believe that Jewish oral law should be the sole constitution of the State. They have, however, failed to create an appropriate instrument for its adaptation to modern conditions of living.

Clannishness rather than unity marks the various orthodox groups. Lacking cohesion, they have failed to realize Rabbi

Maimon's dream of a new Sanhedrin, composed of all the orthodox groupings, to institute reforms which would solve the problem of religion in a modern Jewish state.

6. *Non-Jewish Religions in the State of Israel*

> *For ye know the heart of the stranger, seeing ye were strangers in the land of Egypt.* *Ex. 23:9*

In conformity with this Biblical precept and with the Declaration of the Establishment of the State of Israel, the Government guarantees freedom of faith to all religious minorities within its borders.

Two major non-Judaic world religions are represented in Israel: Christianity and Mohammedanism. As of December 31, 1956, out of a total population of 1,872,390, 45,000 are Christians, 138,000 Moslems.[114]

The main Christian sects are: Greek Catholic, Greek Orthodox, Roman Catholic, Protestant, Maronite, and American Gregorian. The Coptic and Abyssinian Churches are also represented.

The Greek Catholics number some 17,000. Their principal centers are in Galilee.

The Greek Orthodox community numbers some 14,000. It is scattered throughout the towns and villages in the north and south of the country. The higher ranks of the Greek Orthodox hierarchy are priests of Greek origin. Twelve of their monasteries are in Israel territory.

The Roman Catholics number some 5,000. Most of them live in Galilee. From the point of view of their ecclesiastical administration, Israel is divided into the northern area of the country and the southern area.

The Protestants are represented by some 1,200 members. The most important of their Churches is the Anglican, under the authority of the Anglican Bishop in Jerusalem. Almost all of the Protestant Churches are represented by Missions, which are active in the bigger towns. The Scottish Church has a Moderator in the Jerusalem Presbytery.

The Maronite community has about 2,500 members. They live in the principal towns and in Upper Galilee. The center of the community is in Lebanon.

The Coptic Church is represented by 91 members; other Christian Churches, including the Abyssinian, by some 1,600 members.

Of the 45,000 Christians residing in Israel, some 35,000 are Arabs who live in the district of Galilee.[115]

All Christians enjoy every civil and political right and have representatives in the Knesset. They have complete religious autonomy, and their clergy is granted various privileges, such as traveling to Old Jerusalem under Transjordan administration. They have their own religious communities, as does every faith in Israel. Each community has autonomy of its communal, educational, and judicial affairs,[116] and each is headed by a Patriarch or Archbishop.

There are some 138,000 Moslems in Israel. The majority are Arabs. Even before the conclusion of the Armistice Agreements with the Arab States,[117] the Ministry of Religious Affairs set up a special Committee for the Preservation of Moslem Religious Buildings.[118] The Mosques of Ramleh, Haifa, Jaffa, Lydda, Tiberias, and Safed have been restored, others not in actual use closed for preservation. Moslem religious functionaries, which include some 165 preachers, judges, and mosque attendants, are paid by the Ministry of Religious Affairs.[119] The Kadis (Moslem religious judges) have been re-invested with the authority to solemnize marriages in conformity with the law of Islam (*Sharia*)[120] and Israel's Women's Equal Rights Law.[121]

Some 20,000 Druzes[122] also reside in the State of Israel. Their religious personnel is the only one not paid by the Israeli Government, but only because such payment is contrary to the tenets of the Druze faith.

The extent of the freedom enjoyed by every non-Jewish minority is revealed by Paul Blanshard:

> I talked with representatives of almost every minority sect in the country—Roman Catholics, Greek Orthodox, Armenian, Copts, Mohammedans, Scotch Presbyterians, and American Evangelicals, and *they all said* that the new government gives its minorities complete freedom of worship and education.[123]

7. *Need for Religious Reforms*

Israel cannot become a clerical state in the European-Catholic sense, because Mosaism has no centralized structure of religious power. There is, however, no separation of religion and state, and the Government gives religion the traditional place of honor. Most Western-educated Jews object to the extension of religious authority over marriage, divorce, and similar matters of personal status and to the regulations concerning kosher food[124] and Sabbath travel.[125] It is true that the religious groups exercise more than proportional influence. But this situation is due to the fact that, up to the coalition with the General Zionists,[126] the balance of power in the Knesset depended on the cooperation of the religionists, and to the fervent desire of the secular national leaders to avoid a *Kulturkampf.*[127]

The exercise of political authority by religious forces in the Knesset, is, therefore, not so large a problem in Israel as is claimed. There is no formal control of the State because the religious Bloc[128] represents only 14 percent of the electorate and is itself divided into three disparate groups.[129] Whatever power it had came solely from its key position in the coalition Government.[130] The alliance was an uneasy one, and when it collapsed,[131] the break was caused as much by economic issues as by religious disputes. The question of religious education for immigrant children, given as the reason for the break, was really not a serious issue between the religious parties and Mapai.

The religious parties are responsible for certain minor disciplines (such as restriction of Sabbath travel), but these are insignificant compared to the problems which confront Jews in other countries. The Jew in Israel knows that there is no compulsory religious observance, that he is free not to attend the synagogue, not to eat kosher food, not to observe religious holidays.

Still, it cannot be denied that the religious issue divides the people of Israel into two camps. But the division is not so much between religion and secularism as between orthodoxy and less intransigent Judaism. The Jews of Israel revolt not against the religious laws but against a Judaism which does not try to adjust to the spirit of the time, to its ideas, sentiments, and secular knowledge.

The life of modern Jews is based on concepts radically different from those of their parents. This phenomenon was not so conspicuous in exile, for there Jewish life was divided into two parts—the everyday life and the religious life. But in Israel it is not possible to lead two lives, it is all one. The future of orthodox Judaism depends on its success in convincing the people that there are no two ways of life, that daily life and religion are one. Instead, the gap between the spirit and thinking of modern Jews and their religious life widens.

Orthodox Jewry's inability to cope with the problems of a modern state is illustrated by the following:[132]

1. During the 1936-39 disturbances in Palestine, orthodox young men asked the Chief Rabbinate for a ruling on what was permitted, what forbidden to those in military service. No official answer was given, but unofficially the men were told that in all doubtful cases they were to leave the decision to the orthodox authorities.

2. During the same disturbances, principals of the Yeshivoth[133] declared that their students were not to participate in the Hagana.[134] Simultaneously they demanded that the Hagana supply special guards for these students.

3. During World War II, a Jewish Brigade within the British Army was organized.[135] All national organizations, the Chief Rabbinate among them, called for volunteers to this Brigade. The men who answered that call found themselves in a most awkward position, for they had no official ruling on what was or was not permitted under the law of the Torah to those serving in a non-Jewish army. Though there was no explicit statement to that effect, such an attitude on the part of the Rabbinate implied that if there was doubt about the permissiveness of certain services, let the non-orthodox volunteer.

4. During the 1948 siege of Jerusalem there was a paucity of kosher meat, but plenty of pork. An orthodox rabbi demanded that the kosher meat be reserved for the orthodox soldiers. When the aroused Commandant turned to the Chief Rabbinate for a ruling, he received no definite answer.

5. During the battle for Jerusalem, the orthodox authorities persuaded the military personnel to exempt Torah students from military service. Thus, while thousands of Jerusalem citizens lost their lives, the Torah students let others die for them.

6. Use of water and electricity produced on the Sabbath has not been banned by the religious authorities, yet they demand that religious employees in these vital areas be exempt from work on that day. Similarly, these authorities have not prohibited police work on the Sabbath, yet they demand freedom from service on the Sabbath for religious policemen.

7. Orthodox women are prohibited from serving in the army. But in order for these women to eschew military service others must serve for them.

8. Though in some services vital to the community the religious authorities have not proscribed Sabbath work for the unorthodox, they have forbidden Sabbath transportation. That is, when unorthodox practices are to the advantage of the orthodox, the religious authorities refrain from issuing general all-inclusive taboos. Such taboos are however issued in matters

not affecting the needs of the orthodox, such as Sabbath transportation.

9. While demanding that the State of Israel be governed according to the laws of the Torah, the orthodox make no provisions for adapting these laws to modern life.

10. Israel's secular judges guard their political neutrality. They often break party affiliations when appointed. But members of the Chief Rabbinate retain their party affiliations. The Chief Rabbi himself is a member of the National Religious Front (Mizrahi-Hapoel Hamizrahi Party).

In view of the above, certain conclusions are inescapable.

1. To assure kosher meat for the orthodox, the religious practically demand that the non-orthodox eat the forbidden pig meat.

2. To provide the community with water, electricity, and similar services on the Sabbath, the non-religious are to work on that day in order to enable the religious to enjoy all modern conveniences while they rest on the Sabbath.

3. The orthodox are to be exempted from military service, but all others are to serve.

4. To free *their* women from military duty, the orthodox are ready to sacrifice the morals of other women, since, according to their claim, feminine morals are endangered by such service.

5. The orthodox insist that the State be conducted according to the laws of the Torah, but they make no effort to raise the level of Torah-Law studies so as to enable their religious judges to understand the modern world and its problems.

This, then, is Israel's problem: How to conduct affairs of state according to the Torah and at the same time in accordance with the needs of the hour?

Two fundamental viewpoints, contradictory and irreconcilable, face the religious Jew, and he must choose between them. One viewpoint holds that the duty of the Jewish people is to maintain its identity in a Gentile world until the Messiah comes, hence the State of Israel is a rebellion against the Torah. The second insists that Jewish political independence is a religious duty.

The orthodox groups refuse to take a clearcut stand on these basic questions. The Religious Bloc wants the State to remain secular and the traditional religious form to remain intact. They are satisfied to have that form preserved by a religious minority sect (Neturei Karta) within the framework of a secular state, without offering a concrete program for administering the state on religious terms.

The conclusion is inescapable that reform is the answer to Israel's religious problem. Reform means recognition of modern realities; awareness of the points of incompatibility between frozen traditions of antiquity and the technological changes which have transformed man's life; progress and development. Basic changes are the order of the day. Not the changes instituted by the Reform Movement of the last century, which aimed at Jewish assimilation, but changes which will integrate religion and State in Israel and put an end to the conflict between them. A conflict neither side wants.

But it is difficult to introduce even gradual changes, for the religious designate every such attempt as rebellion against, and a danger to, Judaism. Changes *are* a danger to orthodoxy. But what is to be done when orthodoxy's leaders close their eyes to reality and refuse to budge or to permit a natural and necessary religious development to fit our times?

ADDENDA

When, after the third Knesset elections (July, 1955), Ben-Gurion, as prime minister, re-assumed official leadership of the state, the opinion prevailed that in view of the Arab threat—a threat so potently demonstrated in the Sinai campaign of November, 1956—the orthodox-secular truce would continue. But internal events proved that opinion wrong, and led to a break, which culminated, July, 1958, in the orthodox group's departure from the Government. The most important of these events are as follows:

1. Orthodox opposition to the erection of a reform temple in Jerusalem. In 1955 the municipal council of Jerusalem approved the erection of a temple for American reform students by Professor Nelson Gluck, the noted archeologist famed for his discoveries in the Negev. The first to protest a spiritual center for "unbelievers" in the holy city of Jerusalem were of course the Neturei Karta. Though the municipality was not convinced by their and other orthodox arguments, there is still no reform temple in Jerusalem.

2. Orthodox objection to keeping an exhibition open on the Sabbath. The exhibition was being held in completely secular Haifa, the only large city in Israel with public transportation on Saturday. The orthodox organized demonstrations so violent that Haifa's mayor, Aba Chushi, though he fought, was forced by higher authorities to capitulate, de facto if not officially.

3. Orthodoxy's battle against a mixed swimming pool in Jerusalem. Permission was given an Israeli foreign investment firm to build such a pool in that city, where a population of 120,000 has only the facilities of a small YMCA pool. Though the existence of the latter indicates that a mixed swimming pool is not a new idea even to Jerusalem, the orthodox fought bitterly. This time, however—though the demonstrations were

more violent than ever–the Government did not capitulate. The pool is being built–to the delight of the people of Jerusalem.

4. The problem of the definition of a Jew. This question of Jewish identity was the most serious of all, and brought about the defection of the National Religious Front from the Government. I. Bar Jehuda, Minister of the Interior and member of the Achdut Ha'avoda Party, planned to issue new identity cards to all citizens whose racial status was in doubt. The Government decided to define as Jews all who declared themselves to be Jews and who were not members of any other religion. The orthodox fought such a definition, declaring that only the Rabbinical authorities were empowered to rule on this question according to the *Halakha*. The *Halakha* holds that only the progeny of Jewish mothers, or mothers converted to Judaism, are Jews, and that Jewish nationality and religion are inseparable. Certain that this time too the Government would surrender, the orthodox blackmailed it by leaving the coalition. But though, de facto, the Government postponed the issuance of new identity cards, it did not ask them to rejoin it.

This failure to invite the orthodox back into the coalition is considered to be the opening gun in the campaign for the fourth Knesset. The belief prevails that after the election a decisive battle will be waged for the future spirit of Israel. Will it be a state based on the American and Western concept of separation between state and religion? Or will it revert to the Middle Ages, with the Rabbis having the decisive word not in the spiritual realm alone, but, as well, in the political and social? Said Ben-Gurion at a session of Mapai representatives where the question of Jewish definition came up: Rabbi Nissim (Sephardic Chief Rabbi) will not govern the State.

NOTES: PART II

1 "Resolution Adopted in the Report of the Ad Hoc Committee on the Palestinian Question. Plan of Partition with Economic Union (Pt. 1)," *United Nations Resolutions,* September 16-November 29, 1947 (Lake Success: United Nations), pp. 132-133.

2 *Ibid.* "Religious and Minority Rights," p. 137.

3 *Iton Rishmi* (Tel Aviv, Israel: Hapoel-Hatsair), May 14, 1948, p. 2.

4 *Divrei ha-Knesset,* No. 27 (Jerusalem, Israel: Government Printer, June 13, 1950), p. 1743.

5 "The Palestine Order-in-Council, 1922-47," *Constitutions, Laws, Treaties of States in the Near and Middle East,* ed. by Helen Miller Davis (Durham, N. C.: Duke University Press, 1953), pp. 341-357.

6 "Proclamation" [of the Provisional Council of the State of Israel], *Iton Rishmi* (Tel Aviv, Israel: Hapoel-Hatsair), May 14, 1948, p. 3.

7 *Sefer ha'Hukim* [Book of Laws], No. 133 (Jerusalem, Israel: Government Printer, September 3, 1953), p. 165.

8 A Jew who claims descent from the first High Priest of the Jews, Aaron, brother of Moses.

9 Lev. 21:7.

10 *Moezath Hamedinah Hazmanith,* No. 8 (Tel Aviv: Government Printer, July 8, 1948), p. 12.

11 *Divrei ha-Knesset,* No. 27 (Jerusalem, Israel: Government Printer, June 13, 1950), p. 1711.

12 *State of Israel Facts and Figures, 1955* (New York: Israel Office of Information), p. 16.

13 *Sefer ha'Hukim* [Book of Laws], No. 131 (Jerusalem, Israel: Government Printer, August 20, 1953), pp. 137-142.

14 General Federation of Jewish Labor in Israel, founded in 1920 in Haifa.

15 A religious group of the Histadruth.

16 *State of Israel Facts and Figures, 1955* (New York: Israel Office of Information), p. 54.

17 *Ibid.*

18 The Jewish Agency for Palestine, in accordance with Article IV of the League of Nations Mandate for Palestine, was established in Zurich, August, 1929, to advise the Palestine British Government on matters affecting the establishment of a Jewish National Home in Palestine.

19 *Sefer ha'Hukim* [Book of Laws], No. 25 (September 15, 1949), pp. 271-278.

20 *Ibid.,* No. 93 (March 13, 1952), p. 138.

21 *Ibid.,* No. 134 (September 4, 1953), p. 163.
22 *Ibid.,* p. 165
23 *Ibid.,* p. 163.
24 "The Marriage and Divorce Laws," *Jewish Horizon,* XVI (October, 1953), p. 14.
25 *Facts About Israel, 1958, Tenth Anniversary Edition* (New York: Israel Office of Information), April, 1958, p. 44.
26 Observance of Jewish kosher laws.
27 "Legislation and Law in the Jewish State," *Yavneh* (Jerusalem-Tel Aviv, Israel), April-May, 1949, p. 9.
28 Except for the negligible Neturei Karta—a small extremist group of a few hundred souls who live in a special quarter (Me'ah Shearim) of Jerusalem.
29 *Sefer ha'Hukim* [Book of Laws], No. 134 (September 4, 1953), p. 165.
30 "Legislation and Law in the Jewish State," *Yavneh* (Jerusalem-Tel Aviv, Israel), April-May, 1949, p. 9.
31 This is why Rabbi Yitzhak Meir Levin, leader of the Agudat Israel Party, refused the office of Minister of Religious Affairs.
32 Rabbinical schools.
33 Dr. P. Colbi, "The Ministry of Religious Affairs in the State of Israel," *Igereth-Lagolah* (Jerusalem) April-May, 1954, pp. 13-16.
34 "The Statutory Jewish Community," *A Survey of Palestine* (Palestine: Government Printer, 1946), II, 915.
35 An Arabic word meaning the granting, or dedication, of property in trust for a pious purpose.
36 "Order in Council of August 10, 1922," *Constitutions, Electoral Laws, Treaties of States in the Near and Middle East,* ed. by Helen Miller Davis (Durham, N. C.: Duke University Press, 1947), pp. 231-2.
37 Robert Harry Drayton (ed.), *The Laws of Palestine* (London: Government of Palestine, 1934), III, 2133.
38 "Elections of Rabbinical Officers and Rabbis of Local Communities," *Palestine Gazette* (Palestine: Government Printer, April, 1936), IX, 230-34. Va'ad Leumi's functions have been assumed since May 14, 1948 by the Ministry for Religious Affairs of the Israeli State.
39 Descendants of Spanish and Near East Jews.
40 Descendants of European Jews.
41 *Op. cit.*
42 *Ibid.*
43 "Elections of Rabbinical Officers and Rabbis of Local Communities," *Palestine Gazette,* IX, Suppl. 1 (Palestine: Government Printer, April 9, 1936), 230-34.
44 *Ibid.*

45 Moshe Ostrowski, *Irgun ha-Yishuv ha-Yehudi be-Eretz Israel* (Jerusalem: Rubin Mass, 1942), pp. 48-49.

46 *Iton Rishmi* (Tel Aviv, Israel: Hapoel-Hatsair), May 14, 1948, p. 2.

47 Moshe Ostrowski, *Irgun ha-Yishuv ha-Yehudi be-Eretz Israel* (Jerusalem: Rubin Mass, 1942), p. 88.

48 Joseph Burg, "Comments on a Split Bloc," *Jewish Horizon,* XV (November, 1952), 10-11.

49 "The Chief Rabbi Clarifies His Stand," *Jewish Horizon,* XVI (May, 1954), 5.

50 *Dat Yisrael u'Medinath Yisrael* (New York: The Jewish Agency, 1951), p. 17.

51 *Ibid.,* p. 21.

52 Moezath G'dolei ha'Torah (a chief rabbinate of the ultra-orthodox Israeli groups).

53 Joseph Burg, "Comments on a Split Bloc," *Jewish Horizon,* XV (November, 1952), 10-11.

54 "The Status of Religion in Israel," *Jewish Frontier,* XVIII (February, 1951), 20.

55 Urban communities.

56 All definitions from *Facts About Israel* (New York: Israel Office of Information, 1957), pp. 59-62.

57 The religious parties—Agudat Israel, Poalei Agudat Israel, Mizrahi & Hapoel Hamizrahi—voted as a "United Religious Bloc" in the 1949 elections to the first Knesset.

58 There are, in addition, three Arab parties: Israel Arab Democrats Party, Progress and Work, and Agriculture and Development.

59 All election figures from *Facts About Israel* (New York: Israel Office of Information, 1957), p. 53.

60 "The Draft Constitution for Israel," *The Jewish Agency's Digest of Press and Events,* No. 12 (Supplement), December 31, 1948, p. 5.

61 *Ibid.,* Article 16.

62 *Ibid.,* Article 77.

63 *Divrei ha-Knesset,* No. 15 (Jerusalem, Israel: Government Printer, February 20, 1950), pp. 808-12.

64 Z. M. Kerstein, "Baricht fun Rav Kirshblum" [Dispatch from Rabbi Kirshblum] *Mizrahi Weg* (New York), January-February, 1954, p. 3.

65 "Resolution Adopted in the Report of the Ad Hoc Committee on the Palestinian Question. Religious Minority Rights," *United Nations Resolutions, September 16-November 29, 1947* (Lake Success: United Nations), p. 137.

66 *Sefer ha'Hukim* [Book of Laws], No. 131 (Jerusalem, Israel: Government Printer, August 20, 1953), pp. 137-42.

67 *Ibid.,* No. 76, May 22, 1951, p. 205.
68 *Ibid.,* No. 134, September 4, 1953, p. 163.
69 *Ibid.,* No. 133, September 3, 1953, p. 165.
70 Z. M. Kerstein, "Baricht fun Rav Kirshblum" [Dispatch from Rabbi Kirshblum], *Mizrahi Weg* (New York), January-February, 1954, p. 3.
71 *Facts About Israel* (New York: Israel Office of Information, 1957), pp. 42-43.
72 *See* p. 18.
73 *Sefer ha'Hukim* [Book of Laws], No. 133 (Jerusalem, Israel: Government Printer, September 3, 1953), p. 165.
74 *State of Israel Government Yearbook 1953-54* (Jerusalem, Israel: Government Printer), p. 56.
75 *Forward, A Jewish Daily* (New York), December 25, 1954.
76 A Hebrew word meaning ethics. Proverbs 8:10.
77 Religious judges.
78 "How Religious is Israel?" *Jewish Horizon,* XVI (May, 1954), 3.
79 Our young men, i.e., members of Hapoel Hamizrahi.
80 Israeli communal farms.
81 Cooperative villages.
82 Zionist pioneers.
83 State of Israel.
84 Rabbi Issachar Levin, "An Affirmative Program," *Jewish Horizon,* XVI (October, 1953), 3-5.
85 Jewish dispersion after the Exile.
86 Gen. 9:27.
87 "Full Observance of the Law as Basis for Re-Assimilation—Religion and National Unity," *Palestine Post,* October 22, 1948.
88 The Jewish Day of Atonement.
89 Joseph Caro, *Shulhan Arukh.* Vol. *Yorah Deah* (Vilno: Window Ram and Brothers, 1880).
90 The Jewish Community in Israel.
91 Spiritual leader of Reform Judaism in the United States.
92 Spiritual leader of the Neturei Karta.
93 "Compulsory Thinking Not Unity. Religion for the Non-Religious," *Palestine Post,* December 17, 1948.
94 1876-1927.
95 D. Z. Pinkas, "Religion's Place in Israel," *Jewish Horizon,* XIV (November, 1951), 14.
96 *Facts About Israel* (New York: Israel Office of Information, 1957), p. 53.
97 Maurice A. Jaffe, "Are the Israelis Religious?" *Jewish Horizon,* XV (November, 1952), 4.
98 *Iton Rishmi* (Tel Aviv, Israel: Hapoel-Hatsair), May 14, 1948, p. 2.

99 Rabbi Y. M. Levin, Knesset representative of the Agudat Israel, resigned from the Coalition Government September 18, 1952.

100 *Sefer ha'Hukim* [Book of Laws], No. 133 (Jerusalem, Israel: Government Printer, September 3, 1953), p. 165.

101 Dr. Mordecai Nurok [Mizrahi representative in the Knesset] *Divrei ha-Knesset,* No. 27 (Jerusalem, Israel: Government Printer, June 13, 1950), p. 1720.

102 *Forward, A Jewish Daily,* August 15, 1954.

103 *State of Israel Facts and Figures 1954* (New York: Israel Office of Information), p. 16.

104 Hapoel Hamizrahi, Agudat Israel, Poalei Agudat Israel, and Mizrahi parties.

105 *State of Israel Government Yearbook, 1952-53* (Jerusalem, Israel: Government Printer), p. 48.

106 David Ben-Gurion, "Too Many Parties," *Der Tog* (The Day), February 27, 1955, pp. 1-2.

107 *Iton Rishmi,* Supplement 1 (Tel Aviv, Israel: Hapoel-Hatsair), November 26, 1948, p. 62.

108 *Sefer ha'Hukim* [Book of Laws], No. 25 (Jerusalem, Israel: Government Printer, September 15, 1949), pp. 271-8.

109 *Ibid.,* No. 134, September 4, 1953, pp. 163-4.

110 Not until the break of July, 1958 have all the religious parties been in the Opposition.

111 Agudat Israel has its own non-government schools.

112 A good deed which will be rewarded in Heaven—a crusade.

113 The body of Jewish traditions handed down orally from religious master to pupil. Because of this oral nature that law was accepted only by the Pharisees.

114 All figures from *Facts About Israel* (New York: Israel Office of Information, 1957), pp. 49-52.

115 *Zionist Newsletter,* No. 8 (Jerusalem, Israel), January 27, 1953, p. 11.

116 *State of Israel Government Yearbook, 1953-54* (Jerusalem: Government Printer), p. 223.

117 The various armistices were executed as follows:

February 29, 1949—Israel-Egyptian Armistice
March 23, 1949 —Israel-Lebanon Armistice
April 3, 1949 —Israel-Transjordan Armistice
July 20, 1949 —Israel-Syrian Armistice

State of Israel Government Yearbook, 1951-52 (Jerusalem: Government Printer), pp. 255-88.

118 *Ibid.,* 1950-51, p. 191.

119 Rabbi S. Rappaport, "Moslem Religious Institutions in Israel," *Zionist Record Annual* (New Year Annual, 5712), October, 1951, pp. 67-68; *Facts About Israel* (New York: Israel Office of Information), 1957, p. 51.

120 Jurisdiction in matters of Moslem personal status.
121 *Sefer ha'Hukim* [Book of Laws], No. 82 (Jerusalem, Israel: Government Printer, July 26, 1951), p. 1.
122 A religious sect whose faith combines Mosaic Law, the Christian Gospels, the Koran, and other faiths. Their world population is around 86,000. The sect is named for one of its founders—Darasi (996-1021).
123 Paul Blanshard, "Israel: Church and State," *Nation* (May 27, 1950), pp. 520-22.
124 *Iton Rishmi,* No. 34 (Tel Aviv, Israel: Hapoel Hatsair, November 26, 1948), p. 62.
125 *Ibid.,* No. 4, June 6, 1948, p. 12.
126 *State of Israel Government Yearbook, 1953-54,* p. 56.
127 Paul Blanshard, "Israel: Church and State," *Nation* (May 27, 1950), pp. 520-22.
128 A united religious bloc voted in the 1949 elections to the first Knesset.
129 In the third Knesset, Mizrahi and Hapoel Hamizrahi has eleven and Agudat Israel six members.
130 Before the General Zionists joined the Government, December 23, 1952.
131 *State of Israel Government Yearbook, 1951-52* (Jerusalem: Government Printer), p. 55.
132 The incidents described and conclusions drawn are from Yeshayahu Leybovitz, *Torah u'Mytzwoth Byzman Hazeh.* Tel Aviv: Masada, 5614, p. 173.
133 Rabbinical schools.
134 Jewish self-defense during the Palestine Mandatory Period.
135 *British War Office Announcements, Palestine* (New Haven, Conn.: Yale University Press, 1947), p. 1034.

APPENDIXES

1. The Balfour Declaration
2. The Mandate
3. The Palestine Order in Council
4. Declaration of the Establishment of the State of Israel
5. Proclamation
6. Law and Administration Ordinance
7. Defence Army of Israel Ordinance
8. Days of Rest Ordinance
9. Kasher Food for Soldiers Ordinance
10. Transition Law
11. Admission of Israel to Membership in the United Nations
12. Defence Service Law
13. The Knesset Vote June 13, 1950 for a Constitution by Evolution
14. Women's Equal Rights Law
15. State President (Tenure) Law
16. Nationality Law
17. Entry Into Israel Law
18. State Education Law
19. National Service Law
20. Rabbinical Courts Jurisdiction (Marriage and Divorce) Law
21. Penal Law Revision (Abolition of the Death Penalty for Murder) Law

THE BALFOUR DECLARATION

His Majesty's Government view with favour the establishment in Palestine of a national home for the Jewish people, and will use their best endeavours to facilitate the achievement of this object, it being clearly understood that nothing shall be done which may prejudice the civil and religious rights of existing non-Jewish communities in Palestine, or the rights and political status enjoyed by Jews in any other country.

November 2, 1917

THE MANDATE
(Excerpts)

Preamble

The Council of the League of Nations:

Whereas the Principal Allied Powers have agreed, for the purpose of giving effect to the provisions of Article 22 of the Covenant of the League of Nations, to entrust to a Mandatory selected by the said Powers the administration of the territory of Palestine, which formerly belonged to the Turkish Empire, within such boundaries as may be fixed by them; and

Whereas the Principal Allied Powers have also agreed that the Mandatory should be responsible for putting into effect the declaration originally made on November 2nd, 1917, by the Government of His Britannic Majesty, and adopted by the said Powers, in favour of the establishment in Palestine of a national home for the Jewish people, it being clearly understood that nothing should be done which might prejudice the civil and religious rights of existing non-Jewish communities in Palestine, or the rights and political status enjoyed by Jews in any other country; and

Whereas recognition has thereby been given to the historical connection of the Jewish people with Palestine and to the grounds for reconstituting their national home in that country; and

Whereas the Principal Allied Powers have selected His Britannic Majesty as the Mandatory for Palestine; and

Whereas the mandate in respect of Palestine has been formulated in the following terms and submitted to the Council of the League for approval; and

Whereas His Britannic Majesty has accepted the mandate in respect of Palestine and undertaken to exercise it on behalf of the League of Nations in conformity with the following provisions; and

Whereas by the afore-mentioned Article 22 (paragraph 8), it is provided that the degree of authority, control or administration to be exercised by the Mandatory not having been previously agreed upon by the Members of the League, shall be explicitly defined by the Council of the League of Nations;

Confirming the said mandate, defines its terms as follows:

Article 1.

The Mandatory shall have full powers of legislation and of administration, save as they may be limited by the terms of this mandate.

Article 2.

The Mandatory shall be responsible for placing of the country under such political, administrative and economic conditions as will secure the establishment of the Jewish national home, as laid down in the preamble, and the development of self-governing institutions, and also for safeguarding the civil and religious rights of all the inhabitants of Palestine, irrespective of race and religion.

Article 3.

The Mandatory shall, so far as circumstances permit, encourage local autonomy.

Article 4.

An appropriate Jewish agency shall be recognised as a public body for the purpose of advising and co-operating with the Administration of Palestine in such economic, social and other matters as may affect the establishment of the Jewish national home and the interests of the Jewish population in Palestine, and, subject always to the control of the Administration, to assist and take part in the development of the country.

The Zionist organisation, so long as its organisation and constitution are in the opinion of the Mandatory appropriate, shall be recognised as such agency. It shall take steps in consultation with His Britannic Majesty's Government to secure the co-operation of all Jews who are willing to assist in the establishment of the Jewish national home.

Article 6.

The Administration of Palestine, while ensuring that the rights and position of other sections of the population are not prejudiced, shall facilitate Jewish immigration under suitable conditions and shall encourage, in co-operation with the Jewish agency referred to in Article 4, close settlement by Jews on the land, including State lands and waste lands not required for public purposes.

Article 7.

The Administration of Palestine shall be responsible for enacting a nationality law. There shall be included in this law provisions framed so as to facilitate the acquisition of Palestinian citizenship by Jews who take up their permanent residence in Palestine.

Article 18.

The Mandatory shall see that there is no discrimination in Palestine against the nationals of any State Member of the League of Nations (including companies incorporated under its laws) as compared with those of the Mandatory or of any foreign State in matters concerning taxation, commerce or navigation, the exercise of industries or professions, or in the treatment of merchant vessels or civil aircraft. Similarly, there shall be no discrimination in Palestine against goods originating in or destined for any of the said States, and there shall be freedom of transit under equitable conditions across the mandated area.

Subject as aforesaid and to the other provisions of this mandate, the Administration of Palestine may, on the advice of the Mandatory, impose such taxes and customs duties as it may consider necessary, and take such steps as it may think best to promote the development of the natural resources of the country and to safeguard the interests of the population. It may also, on the advice of the Mandatory, conclude a special customs agreement with any State the territory of which in 1914 was wholly included in Asiatic Turkey or Arabia.

Article 22.

English, Arabic and Hebrew shall be the official languages of Palestine. Any statement or inscription in Arabic on stamps or money in Palestine shall be repeated in Hebrew, and any statement or inscription in Hebrew shall be repeated in Arabic.

Article 23.

The Administration of Palestine shall recognise the holy days of the respective communities in Palestine as legal days of rest for the members of such communities.

Article 25.

In the territories lying between the Jordan and the eastern boundary of Palestine as ultimately determined, the Mandatory shall be entitled, with the consent of the Council of the League of Nations, to postpone or withhold application of such provisions of this mandate as he may consider inapplicable to the existing local conditions, and to make such provision for the administration of the territories as he may consider suitable to those conditions, provided that no action shall be taken which is inconsistent with the provisions of Articles 15, 16 and 18.

Article 27.

The consent of the Council of the League of Nations is required for any modification of the terms of this mandate.

July 24, 1922

THE PALESTINE ORDER IN COUNCIL
(Excerpts)

Art. 53. The Rabbinical Court of the Jewish Community shall have:

(1) Exclusive jurisdiction in matters of marriage and divorce, alimony and confirmation of wills of members of their community other than foreigners as defined in Article 59.

(2) Jurisdiction in any other matter of personal status of such persons, where all the parties to the action consent to their jurisdiction.

(3) Exclusive jurisdiction over any case as to the constitution or internal administration of a wakf or religious endowment constituted before the Rabbinical Court according to Jewish law.

Art. 59. For the purpose of this part of the Order, the expression "foreigner" means any person who is not a Palestinian citizen.

August 10, 1922

DECLARATION OF THE ESTABLISHMENT OF THE STATE OF ISRAEL

Eretz Israel was the birthplace of the Jewish people. Here their spiritual, religious and political identity was shaped. Here they first attained to statehood, created cultural values of national and universal significance and gave to the world the eternal Book of Books.

After being forcibly exiled from their land, the people kept faith with it throughout their Dispersion and never ceased to pray and hope for their return to it and for the restoration in it of their political freedom.

Impelled by this historic and traditional attachment, Jews strove in every successive generation to re-establish themselves in their ancient homeland. In recent decades they returned in their masses. Pioneers, *ma'pilim* and defenders, they made deserts bloom, revived the Hebrew language, built villages and towns, and created a thriving community, controlling its own economy and culture, loving peace but knowing how to defend itself, bringing the blessings of progress to all the country's inhabitants, and aspiring towards independent nationhood.

In the year 5657 (1897), at the summons of the spiritual father of the Jewish State, Theodor Herzl, the First Zionist Congress convened and proclaimed the right of the Jewish people to national rebirth in its own country.

This right was recognized in the Balfour Declaration of the 2nd November, 1917, and re-affirmed in the Mandate of the League of Nations which, in particular, gave international sanction to the historic connection between the Jewish people and Eretz-Israel and to the right of the Jewish people to rebuild its National Home.

The catastrophe which recently befell the Jewish people—the massacre of millions of Jews in Europe—was another clear demonstration of the urgency of solving the problem of its homelessness by re-establishing in Eretz-Israel the Jewish State, which would open the gates of the homeland wide to every

Jew and confer upon the Jewish people the status of a fully-privileged member of the comity of nations.

Survivors of the Nazi holocaust in Europe, as well as Jews from other parts of the world, continued to migrate to Eretz-Israel, undaunted by difficulties, restrictions and dangers, and never ceased to assert their right to a life of dignity, freedom and honest toil in their national homeland.

In the Second World War, the Jewish community of this country contributed its full share to the struggle of the freedom- and peace-loving nations against the forces of Nazi wickedness and, by the blood of its soldiers and its war effort, gained the right to be reckoned among the people who founded the United Nations.

On the 29th November, 1947, the United Nations General Assembly passed a resolution calling for the establishment of a Jewish State in Eretz-Israel; the General Assembly required the inhabitants of Eretz-Israel to take such steps as were necessary on their part for the implementation of that resolution. This recognition by the United Nations of the right of the Jewish people to establish their State is irrevocable.

This right is the natural right of the Jewish people to be masters of their own fate, like all other nations, in their own sovereign State.

Accordingly We, Members of the People's Council, Representatives of the Jewish Community of Eretz-Israel and of the Zionist Movement, Are Here Assembled on the Day of the Termination of the British Mandate Over Eretz-Israel and, by Virtue of Our Natural and Historic Right and on the Strength of the Resolution of the United Nations General Assembly, Hereby Declare the Establishment of a Jewish State in Eretz-Israel, to Be Known as the State of Israel.

We Declare that, with effect from the moment of the termination of the Mandate, being tonight, the eve of Sabbath, the 6th Iyar, 5708 (15th May, 1948), until the establishment of the elected, regular authorities of the State in accordance with the Constitution which shall be adopted by the Elected Constituent Assembly not later than the 1st October, 1948, the People's Council shall act as a Provisional Council of State, and its executive organ, the People's Administration, shall be the Provisional Government of the Jewish State, to be called "Israel."

The State of Israel will be open for Jewish immigration and for the Ingathering of the Exiles; it will foster the development of the country for the benefit of all inhabitants; it will be based on freedom, justice and peace as envisaged by the prophets of Israel; it will ensure complete equality of social and political rights to all its inhabitants irrespective of religion, race or sex; it will guarantee freedom of religion, conscience, language, education and culture; it will safeguard the Holy Places of all religions; and it will be faithful to the principles of the Charter of the United Nations.

The State of Israel is prepared to cooperate with the agencies and representatives of the United Nations in implementing the resolution of the General Assembly of the 29th November, 1947, and will take steps to bring about the economic union of the whole of Eretz-Israel.

We Appeal to the United Nations to assist the Jewish people in the building-up of its State and to receive the State of Israel into the comity of nations.

We Appeal—in the very midst of the onslaught launched against us now for months—to the Arab inhabitants of the State of Israel to preserve peace and participate in the upbuilding of the State on the basis of full and equal citizenship and due representation in all its provisional and permanent institutions.

We Extend our hand to all neighbouring states and their peoples in an offer of peace and good neighbourliness, and appeal to them to establish bonds of cooperation and mutual help with the sovereign Jewish people settled in its own land. The State of Israel is prepared to do its share in common effort for the advancement of the entire Middle East.

We Appeal to the Jewish people throughout the Diaspora to rally round the Jews of Eretz-Israel in the tasks of immigration and upbuilding and to stand by them in the great struggle for the realization of the age-old dream—the redemption of Israel.

Placing Our Trust in the Almighty, We Affix Our Signatures to This Proclamation at This Session of the Provisional Council of State, on the Soil of the Homeland, in the City of Tel-Aviv, on This Sabbath Eve, the 5th Day of Iyar, 5708 (14th May, 1948).

(For signatures, except of Dr. Chaim Weizmann, see page 87.)

PROCLAMATION

In virtue of the Declaration of Independence published this day, the fifth of Iyar, five thousand seven hundred and eight (14th May, 1948), under which the Provisional Council of State and the Provisional Government of the State of Israel have been constituted, the Provisional Council of State hereby declares as follows:

1. The Provisional Council of State is the legislative authority. The Provisional Council of State is entitled to delegate some of its legislative power to the Provisional Government for the purpose of urgent legislation.

2. Such provisions of the law as arise from the White Paper of 1939 are hereby declared null and void.

Sections 13 to 15 of the Immigration Ordinance, 1941, and Regulations 102 to 107C of the Defence (Emergency) Regulations, 1945, are hereby repealed.

The Land Transfers Regulations, 1940, are hereby repealed retroactively as from the 29th Iyar, 5699 (18th May, 1939).

3. So long as no laws have been enacted by or on behalf of the Provisional Council of State, the law which existed in

Palestine on the 5th Iyar, 5708 (14th May, 1948) shall continue in force in the State of Israel, insofar as such continuance in force is consistent with the contents of this Proclamation, with the future laws and with the changes arising from the establishment of the State and its authorities.

May 14, 1948

LAW AND ADMINISTRATION ORDINANCE

No. 1 of 5708–1948

By virtue of the power conferred upon the Provisional Council of the State by the Declaration of the Establishment of the State of Israel, of the 5th Iyar, 5708 (14th May, 1948) and by the Proclamation of that date, the Provisional Council of the State hereby enacts as follows:

Chapter One: The Administration

1. (a) The Provisional Council of the State consists of the persons whose names are set out in the Schedule of this Ordinance. Representatives of Arabs being residents of the State who recognize the State of Israel will be co-opted on the Provisional Council of the State, as may be decided by the Council; their non-participation in the Council shall not derogate from its power.

(b) The Provisional Council of State itself prescribes the procedure for its business and meetings.

2. (a) The Provisional Government consists of the persons whose names are set out in the Schedule to this Ordinance. Representatives of Arabs being residents of the State who recognize the State of Israel will be co-opted on the Provisional Government, as may be decided by the Provisional Council of the State; their non-participation in the Provisional Government shall not derogate from its power.

(b) The Provisional Government shall act in accordance with the policy laid down by the Provisional Council of State, shall carry out its decisions, shall report to it on its activities and shall be answerable to the Provisional Council of State for its activities.

(c) The Provisional Government shall elect one of its members to be Prime Minister, and shall prescribe the functions of each of its members. A member of the Provisional Government shall be called "Minister."

(d) The Provisional Government may confer any of its powers upon the Prime Minister and upon any of the Ministers in so far as that it is not repugnant to the Ordinances of the Provisional Council of State.

(e) Decisions of the Provisional Government in respect of the functions of its members and in respect of the division of powers among the Ministers shall be published in the Official Gazette.

(f) The Provisional Government itself prescribes the procedure for its meetings and business.

3. The Provisional Government may divide the area of the State into districts and sub-districts and shall demarcate their boundaries.

4. The municipal corporation, local councils and other local authorities shall continue to act within the areas of their jurisdiction and scope of their authority.

Chapter Two: Budget and Taxes

5. The budget of the Provisional Government shall be affixed by an Ordinance of the Provisional Council of State.

6. No Government taxes or other obligatory payments to Government the imposition whereof has not been authorized by law may be imposed, and no Government taxes or obligatory

payments to Government the imposition whereof is authorized by law, may be increased, save in accordance with an Ordinance of the Provisional Council of State.

Chapter Three: Legislation

7. (a) The Provisional Council of State is the legislative authority. The laws shall be called "Ordinances."

(b) Every Ordinance shall be signed by the Prime Minister, the Minister of Justice and the Minister or Ministers charged with the implementation of the Ordinance.

8. Each Minister may make regulations for the implementation of the Ordinances which are within the scope of his authority, insofar as such Ordinances confer power to make regulations.

9. (a) If the Provisional Council of State deems it expedient so to do, it may declare that a state of emergency exists in the State, and upon such declaration being published in the Official Gazette, the Provisional Government may authorize the Prime Minister to make such Emergency Regulations as may seem to him expedient in the interests of the defence of the State, public security and the maintenance of supplies and essential services.

(b) An Emergency Regulation may alter any law, suspend its effect or modify it, and may also impose or increase taxes or other obligatory payments.

(c) An Emergency Regulation shall expire three months after it is made, unless it is extended, or revoked at an earlier date, by an Ordinance of the Provisional Council of State or revoked by the regulation-making authority.

(d) Whenever the Provisional Council of State thinks fit, it shall declare that the state of emergency has ceased to exist, and upon such declaration being published in the Official

Gazette, the Emergency Regulations shall expire on the date or dates prescribed in such declaration.

10. (a) Every Ordinance shall come into force on the date of its publication in the Official Gazette, unless it has been provided therein that it shall come into force on an earlier or a later date than the date of publication. The date of the Official Gazette is deemed to be the date of publication.

(b) The publication of an Ordinance in the Official Gazette shall evidence that such Ordinance has been duly enacted and signed.

(c) The Provisions of this section apply also to rules and Emergency Regulations.

Chapter Four: The Law

11. The law which existed in Palestine on the 5th Iyar, 5708 (14th May, 1948) shall remain in force, insofar as there is nothing therein repugnant to this Ordinance or to the other laws which may be enacted by or on behalf of the Provisional Council of State, and subject to such modifications as may result from the establishment of the State and its authorities.

12. (a) Any privilege granted by law to the British Crown, British officials or British subjects, is hereby declared to be null and void.

(b) Any provision in the law whereunder approval or consent of any of the Secretaries of State of the King of England is required or which imposes a duty to do anything in pursuance of his directions is hereby declared to be null and void.

(c) Any power assigned by the law to judges, officers or members of the Police Force by reason of their being British, shall henceforth vest in judges, officers or members of the Police Force who are holders of the same office or rank in the State of Israel.

13. (a) Sections 13 to 15 of the Immigration Ordinance, 1941, and Regulations 102 to 107C of the Defence (Emergency) Regulations, 1945, are hereby repealed. Any Jew who at any time entered Palestine in contravention of the laws of the Mandatory Government shall, for all intents and purposes, be deemed to be a legal immigrant retroactively from the date of his entry into Palestine.

(b) The Land Transfers Regulations, 1940, are hereby repealed retroactively from the 29th Iyar, 5699 (18th May, 1939). No judgment given on the basis of such Regulations shall be a bar to the lodging of a new claim in the same matter.

14. (a) Any power vested under the law in the King of England or in any of his Secretaries of State, and any power vested under the law in the High Commissioner, the High Commissioner in Council, or the Government of Palestine, shall henceforth vest in the Provisional Government, unless such power has been vested in the Provisional Council of State by any of its Ordinances.

(b) Any power vested under the law in British consuls, British consular officers or British passport control officers, shall henceforth vest in consuls and officers to be appointed for that purpose by the Provisional Government.

15. (a) "Palestine," wherever appearing in the law, shall henceforth be read as "Israel."

(b) Any provision in the law requiring the use of the English language is repealed.

16. The Minister of Justice may issue a new text of any law which existed in Palestine on the 5th Iyar, 5708 (14 May, 1948) and which is still in force in the State. Such text shall contain all the modifications resulting from the establishment of the State and its authorities, and upon its publication in the Official Gazette no other text of such law shall have effect.

Chapter Five: Law Courts

17. So long as no new law concerning law courts has been enacted, the law courts existing in the territory of the State shall continue to function within the scope of the powers conferred upon them by law.

Chapter Six: Armed Forces

18. The Provisional Government may establish armed forces on land, on the sea and in the air, which shall have authority to do all lawful and necessary acts for the defence of the State.

Chapter Seven: Transitional Provisions

19. (a) Any order, direction, notice, demand, certificate, instrument, authorization, licence, patent, design, trademark and any other right or concession, and any debt, obligation or liability made, given or imposed by the High Commissioner, the High Commissioner in Council, the Government of Palestine or its authorities or officers, and which was in force in the territory of the State on the 5th Iyar, 5708 (14th May, 1948), shall continue in force until varied, amended or revoked, unless otherwise provided in any of the Ordinances of the Provisional Council of State.

(b) Regulations, orders, notices and directions published, between the 16th Kislev, 5708 (29th November, 1947) and the date of publication of this Ordinance, by the Jewish Agency for Palestine, the General Council (Va'ad Leumi) of the Jewish Community in Palestine, the People's Administration, or by any of their departments, in order to secure the maintenance of supplies and essential services or other economic objects, shall continue in force until varied, amended or revoked by or on behalf of the Provisional Council of State.

20. (a) Any company, partnership or cooperative society which on the 5th Iyar, 5708 (14th May, 1948) was registered in Palestine and which had on that date a registered office or

place of business in the territory of the State, shall henceforth be deemed to be registered in the State.

(b) Any company, partnership or cooperative society which on the 5th Iyar, 5708 (14th May, 1948) was registered in Palestine but did not have on that date a registered office or place of business in the territory of the State, may apply for its registration in the State without payment of fees within three months from the date of publication of this Ordinance.

(c) This section also applies mutatis mutandis to societies under Ottoman Law of Societies, registered business names, and registered ships.

(d) The Minister of Justice shall make regulations for the implementation of this section.

21. The taxes and payments of every kind whatsoever which had not been paid to the Government of Palestine by the 5th Iyar, 5708 (14th May, 1948) shall be paid to the Provisional Government.

22. This Ordinance may be cited as the Law and Administration Ordinance, 5708–1948.

23. This Ordinance shall have effect retroactively as from the eve of the Sabbath, 6th Iyar, 5708 (15th May, 1948),

and its provisions amplify and interpret the provisions of the Proclamation of the Provisional Council of the State of the 5th Iyar, 5708 (14th May, 1948).

Schedule

Members of the Provisional Council of State:

Dr. Chaim Weizmann
David Ben-Gurion

Daniel Auster
Eliyahu Berligne
Meir Grabovsky
Eliyahu Dobkin
Rachel Cohen
Rabbi Itzhak Meir Levin
Golda Myerson
Zvi Segal
Aharon Zisling
Dr. Abraham Katznelson
Berl Repetur
Bechor Shalom Shitreet

Mordechai Bentov
Fritz Bernstein
Yitzhak Gruenbaum
Herzl Vardi
Rabbi Kalman Kahana
Meir David Loewenstein
Shmuel Mikunis
Rabbi Yehuda Leib Hacohen-Fishman
Moshe Kolodny
Felix Rosenblueth
Moshe Shapira
Mordechai Shattner

Yitzhak Ben Zvi
Rabbi Wolf Gold
Dr. Abraham Granovsky
Zerah Wahrhaftig
Saadia Kobashi
Zvi Luria
Nahum Nir-Rafalkes
David Zvi Pinkas
Eliezer Kaplan
David Remez
Ben-Zion Sternberg
Moshe Shertok

Members of the Provisional Government

David Ben-Gurion

Mordechai Bentov
Rabbi Yitzhak Meir Levin
Eliezer Kaplan
Bechor Shalom Shitreet

Fritz Bernstein
Rabbi Yehuda Leib Hacohen-Fishman
Moshe Shertok
Felix Rosenblueth

Moshe Shapira
Yitzhak Gruenbaum
Aharon Zisling
David Remez

May 19, 1948

DEFENCE ARMY OF ISRAEL ORDINANCE

No. 4 of 5708–1948

An Ordinance Establishing a Defence Army of the State of Israel

By virtue of section 18 of the Law and Administration Ordinance, 5708–1948, the following Ordinance is hereby enacted:

1. There is hereby established a Defence Army of Israel, consisting of land forces, a navy and an air force.

2. In a state of emergency there shall be introduced compulsory enlistment for all the services of the Defence Army of Israel.

The age of those liable to enlistment shall be as shall be prescribed by the Provisional Government.

3. Every person serving in the Defence Army of Israel shall take an oath of allegiance to the State of Israel, its Constitution and its competent authorities.

4. It is forbidden to establish or maintain any armed force outside the Defence Army of Israel.

5. Orders, declarations, regulations and any other directions concerning matters of the national service which were published by the Jewish Agency for Palestine, the General Council (Va'ad Leumi) of the Jewish Community of Palestine, the People's Administration, the Provisional Government or any of their departments between the 16th Kislev, 5708 (29th November, 1947) and the date of publication of this Ordinance, shall remain in force so long as they have not been varied, amended or revoked.

6. Any act done in accordance with the provisions of this Ordinance shall be legal, even if it is repugnant to any other provision in the existing law.

7. The Minister of Defence is charged with the implementation of this Ordinance.

8. This Ordinance may be cited as the Defence Army of Israel Ordinance, 5708–1948.

May 26, 1948

DAYS OF REST ORDINANCE

No. 6 of 5708–1948

The Provisional Council of State hereby enacts as follows:

1. The Sabbath and the Jewish festivals, namely the two days of New Year, the Day of Atonement, the first day of the Feast of Tabernacles and the Eighth Day of Solemn Assembly, the first and seventh days of Passover and the Feast of Pentecost, shall be the prescribed days of rest in the State of Israel.

Non-Jews shall have the right to observe their own Sabbath and festivals as days of rest.

2. The above provision shall form part of the Law and Administration Ordinance, 5708–1948, and shall be inserted in it, under the heading "Chapter Six A: Days of Rest," as section 18A.

3. This Ordinance shall have retroactive effect from the night of Sabbath, the 6th Iyar, 5708 (15th May, 1948).

4. This Ordinance may be cited as the Days of Rest Ordinance, 5708–1948.

June 3, 1948

KASHER FOOD FOR SOLDIERS ORDINANCE

No. 14 of 5709–1948

The Provisional Council of State hereby enacts as follows:

1. The supply of *kasher* food shall be ensured to all Jewish soldiers of the Defence Army of Israel.

2. The Minister of Defence and the Minister of Religious Affairs are charged with the implementation of this Ordinance.

3. This Ordinance shall come into force on the 16th Cheshvan, 5709 (18th November, 1948).

4. This Ordinance may be cited as the *Kasher* Food for Soldiers Ordinance, 5709–1948.

November 25, 1948

TRANSITION LAW, 5709–1949
(Small Constitution)

Chapter One: The Knesset

1. The legislative body of the State of Israel shall be called the Knesset. The Constituent Assembly shall be called "The First Knesset." A delegate to the Constituent Assembly shall be called "a member of the Knesset."

2. (a) An enactment of the Knesset shall be called a Law.

(b) Every Law shall be signed by the Prime Minister and by the Minister or Ministers charged with its implementation.

(c) The President of the State shall sign every Law, except Laws concerning his powers.

(d) Every Law shall be published in the *State Records* within ten days from the date of its being passed by the Knesset.

Chapter Two: The President of the State

3. (a) The President of the State shall be elected by the Knesset by secret ballot. (*See* State President (Tenure) Law, page 103.)

(b) The candidate who obtains the votes of more than half of all the members of the Knesset shall be considered elected.

(c) If no candidate obtains a majority of votes as aforesaid, there shall be a second ballot. If no such majority is obtained in the second ballot, voting shall continue, and in the third and any further ballot, the candidate who obtained the smallest number of votes in the preceding ballot shall not stand again for election. The candidate who in the third or any further ballot obtains the votes of more than half of the members of the Knesset taking part in the ballot shall be considered elected.

4. Within seven days of his election, the President shall make and sign in the Knesset, or before the Chairman of the Knesset, the following declaration:

"I, (name), pledge myself as President of the State, to be loyal to the State of Israel and to its Laws."

5. The President of the State shall hold office for the duration of the term of office of the First Knesset and until the expiration of three months from the convening of the new Knesset.

6. The President of the State shall sign treaties with foreign states which have been ratified by the Knesset, appoint, upon the recommendation of the competent Minister, the diplomatic representatives of the State, receive diplomatic representatives of foreign states who have been sent to Israel, and approve the appointment of consuls of foreign states; he shall also be empowered to pardon offienders and to reduce punishments.

7. Every official document signed by the President of the State shall be countersigned by the Prime Minister or by such other Minister as may be designated in that behalf by the Government.

Chapter Three: The Government

8. Immediately upon the election of the President of the State, the Provisional Government shall tender to him its resignation, but it shall continue to exercise its functions pending the constitution of a new Government.

9. After consultation with representatives of the party groups within the Knesset, the President of the State shall entrust a member of the Knesset with the task of forming a Government.

10. The Government shall consist of the Prime Minister and of a number of Ministers, who may or may not be members of the Knesset.

11. (a) As soon as the Government has been formed, it shall present itself to the Knesset, and after having obtained a vote of confidence, it shall be considered as constituted.

(b) Within seven days of the date on which the Government obtains such a vote of confidence, the Prime Minister and the other Ministers shall read and sign before the Knesset the following declaration:

"I, (name), as a member of the Government, pledge myself to be loyal to the State of Israel and to its laws, and to comply with the decisions of the Knesset."

(c) The Government shall be jointly responsible for its activities to the Knesset, shall report to it on its activities, and shall hold office as long as it enjoys the confidence of the Knesset.

(d) A Government which receives a vote of non-confidence from the Knesset, or which has decided to resign, shall immediately tender its resignation to the President of the State, but it shall continue to exercise its functions pending the constitution of a new Government in accordance with the provisions of this Law.

Chapter Four: Further Provisions

12. The Government shall have all the powers vested by law in the Provisional Government.

13. Everything required by law to be published in the *Official Gazette* shall henceforward be published in the *State Records;*

every reference in the law to the *Official Gazette* shall henceforward be deemed to be a reference to the *State Records.*

14. Section 1 (c) and (d), section 2 (b) and (c), the second sentence of section 7 (a), and section 7 (b), of the Law and Administration Ordinance, 5708–1948, are hereby repealed.

15. This Law shall have effect from the date of its being passed by the Knesset.

February 16, 1949

ADMISSION OF ISRAEL TO MEMBERSHIP IN THE UNITED NATIONS

Having received the report of the Security Council on the application of Israel for membership in the United Nations,

Noting that, in the judgment of the Security Council, Israel is a peace-loving State and is able and willing to carry out the obligations contained in the Charter,

Noting that the Security Council has recommended to the General Assembly that it admit Israel to membership in the United Nations,

Noting furthermore the declaration by the State of Israel that it "unreservedly accepts the obligations of the United Nations Charter and undertakes to honour them from the day when it becomes a Member of the United Nations,"

Recalling its resolutions of 29 November 1947 and 11 December 1948 and taking note of the declarations and explanations made by the representative of the Government of Israel before the *ad hoc* Political Committee in respect of the implementation of the said resolutions,

The General Assembly,

Acting in discharge of its functions under Article 4 of the Charter and rule 125 of its rules of procedure,

1. *Decides* that Israel is a peace-loving State which accepts the obligations contained in the Charter and is able and willing to carry out those obligations;

2. *Decides* to admit Israel to membership in the United Nations.

May 11, 1949

DEFENCE SERVICE LAW, 5709–1949
(Excerpts)

1. In this Law–
"defence service" means–

(a) service in the Regular Forces of the Defence Army of Israel (hereinafter: "regular service");

(b) service in the Reserve Forces of the Defence Army of Israel (hereinafter: "reserve service");

"ordinary resident" means a person whose ordinary place of residence is within the territory in which the law of the State of Israel applies;

"person of military age" means an ordinary resident of an age as specified hereunder:

(a) in the case of a male person–any age from eighteen to forty-nine years inclusive;

(b) in the case of a female person–any age from eighteen to thirty-four years inclusive.

2. For the purposes of this Law, a person attaining a particular age in a particular year of the Hebrew calendar shall be deemed to attain such age on the 1st of Nissan of such year.

3. (a) The Minister of Defence may appoint a calling-up officer or calling-up officers for the purpose of this Law.

(b) The appointment of a calling-up officer may be either general or restricted.

(c) Notice of the appointment of a calling-up officer shall be published in the *State Records*.

4. (a) A calling-up officer may, by order, call upon any person of military age to report for registration at such place and time as shall be fixed in the order.

(b) A person of military age who has been called upon to report as aforesaid shall report at the place and time fixed in the order and give the calling-up officer, or a person appointed by him in that behalf, such particulars relating to himself as shall be determined by regulations.

(c) Where a person of military age is called upon to report as aforesaid and, after he has fulfilled his obligations under subsection (b), a change occurs in one of the particulars referred to in subsection (b), such particular having been defined by regulations as a material particular, such person shall notify the calling-up officer of such change within thirty days of the day on which it occurred.

(d) A calling-up officer may, by order, call upon an ordinary resident of seventeen years of age to report for registration at such place and time as shall be fixed in the order. Upon such order being issued, subsections (b) and (c) shall apply to such ordinary resident as though he were a person of military age.

5. (a) A calling-up officer may, by order, call upon any person of military age to report, at such place and time as shall be fixed in the order, for medical examination with a view to ascertaining his medical fitness for defence service.

(b) A person of military age who has been called upon to report as aforesaid shall report at the place and time fixed in the order and be subjected by a medical board to any examination which, in the opinion of the board, is necessary to ascertain his medical fitness for defence service. The tests for the various grades of medical fitness shall be prescribed by regulations.

(c) When a medical board has completed the examination of a person of military age, it shall state whether it finds such person medically fit for defence service (hereinafter: "fit for service") or medically unfit for defence service (hereinafter: "unfit for service").

(d) A person of military age whom a medical board has found fit for service or unfit for service, as the case may be, may on such conditions as may be prescribed by regulations, request that a higher medical board subject him to a further medical examination and state whether it finds him fit for service or unfit for service.

(e) The mode of setting-up and rules of procedure of a medical board and a higher medical board shall be prescribed by regulations.

6. (a) A calling-up officer may, by order, call upon—

(1) a male person of military age who has been found fit for service and is of any age from eighteen years to twenty-nine years inclusive, and

(2) a female person of military age who has been found fit for service and who is of any age from eighteen years to twenty-six years inclusive,

to report, within the periods specified in subsection (d) and at such place and time as shall be fixed in the order, for regular service, and such person shall report accordingly.

(b) A male person of military age who has been called upon to report for regular service under subsection (a), shall be liable to regular service—

(1) if he was called upon to report for regular service while being of any age from eighteen years to twenty-six years inclusive—for a period of twenty-four months;

(2) if he was called upon to report for regular service while being of any age from twenty-seven years to twenty-nine years inclusive—for a period of eighteen months.

(c) A female person of military age who has been called upon to report for regular service under subsection (a) shall be liable to regular service for a period of twelve months.

(d) A person of military age shall not be called upon to report for regular service unless the time fixed for such reporting is within a period as specified hereunder—

(1) if on the date of the coming into force of this Law such person is of any age from eighteen years to twenty-five years inclusive—within twenty-four months of the date of the coming into force of this Law;

(2) if on the date of the coming into force of this Law such person is of any age from twenty-six years to twenty-nine years inclusive—within twelve months of the date of the coming into force of this Law;

(3) if such person attains the age of eighteen years after the coming into force of this Law—within twenty-four months after his attaining the age of eighteen years;

(4) if such person arrives in the country as an immigrant (*oleh*) after the coming into force of this Law—within such period as shall be fixed by regulations.

(e) Notwithstanding anything contained in subsection (d), a person of military age whose regular service has been postponed upon his application in accordance with section 12 may be called upon to report for regular service if the time fixed for such reporting is within twelve months of the date of expiration of the period of postponement.

(f) The first twelve months of the regular service of a male person and the twelve months of the regular service of a female person shall, after basic military training, be devoted mainly to agricultural training, as shall be prescribed by regulations: Provided that the Minister of Defence may, in respect of a person of military age who has stated his desire to serve, and has been accepted for service, in the Air Force or the Navy, direct that the period of service of such person assigned for agricultural training shall be devoted, wholly or in part, to service in the Air Force or the Navy, as the case may be. The branches of farming the training in which shall be considered as agricultural training, and the order and regime of agricultural training, shall be prescribed by regulations.

(g) The Minister of Defence shall make regulations with a view to safeguarding, in carrying into effect the provisions of this section, the integrity of settlement nuclei.

(h) The Minister of Defence shall make regulations with a view to regulating the fulfilment of the obligation of regular service by persons of military age who arrive in the country as immigrants (*olim*) after the coming into force of this Law.

(i) Notwithstanding anything contained in this section—

(1) any person of military age who, immediately before the coming into force of this law, was serving on full-time service in the Defence Army of Israel, shall be liable to regular service for a period of twenty-four months or such shorter period as the Minister of Defence may direct;

(2) a person of military age who, before the coming into force of this Law, was discharged from full-time service in the Defence Army of Israel after military service of one year or over, shall not be called upon to report for regular service under this section.

(j) Where a person of military age liable to regular service has served on military service during the period from the 19th

Tevet, 5708 (1st January, 1948) to the date of the coming into force of this Law, the period of his military service shall be deducted from the period of regular service to which he is liable.

(k) In this section, "military service" means—

(1) in respect of the period from the 19th Tevet, 5708 (1st January, 1948) to the 21st Iyar, 5708 (30th May, 1948)—any service which the Minister of Defence may, by declaration published in the *State Records,* declare to be military service for the purpose of this section;

(2) in respect of the period from the 22nd Iyar, 5708 (31st May, 1948) to the date of the coming into force of this Law—full-time service in the Defence Army of Israel.

7. (a) A person of military age who has been found fit for service and who is not serving on regular service, shall belong to the Reserve Forces of the Defence Army of Israel and shall be liable to reserve service as specified hereunder:

(1) in the case of a male person of any age from eighteen years to thirty-nine years inclusive, and in the case of a female person of any age from eighteen years to thirty-four years inclusive—for a period not exceeding thirty-one consecutive days of service each year plus one day of service each month: Provided that such day shall not fall on a Sabbath or Jewish religious holiday;

(2) in the case of a male person of any age from forty years to forty-nine years inclusive—for a period not exceeding fourteen consecutive days of service each year plus one day of service each month: Provided that such day shall not fall on Sabbath or a Jewish religious holiday;

(3) in the case of a commander—for a period not exceeding seven consecutive days of service in addition to the consecutive days of service referred to in paragraphs (1) and (2); in this paragraph, "commander" means any

person of military age, whether male or female, of or above the rank of full corporal in the Land Forces or of or above the corresponding rank in the Air Force or the Navy.

(b) A calling-up officer may, by order, call upon a person of military age liable to reserve service as aforesaid to report for reserve service at such place and time as shall be fixed in the order, and such person of military age shall report accordingly.

8. (a) The Minister of Defence may, if he is satisfied that the security of the State so requires, call, by order, upon any person of military age who belongs to the Reserve Forces of the Defence Army of Israel to report for regular service or reserve service, as shall be specified in the order, at such place and time as shall be fixed therein, and to serve so long as the order shall be in force; and such person of military age shall report and serve accordingly.

(b) An order issued under subsection (a) shall, as soon as possible after it is issued, be brought by the Minister of Defence to the notice of the Knesset Committee on Security and Foreign Affairs. The Committee may confirm the order, with or without modifications, or refuse to confirm it or place it before the Knesset. The order shall expire fourteen days after the date of its issue, except if, and as, confirmed by the Committee or the Knesset prior to the termination of the said period.

9. Rules to be followed by calling-up officers when issuing orders calling upon persons of military age to report under this Law, and rules as to the procedure for such reporting, shall be prescribed by regulations.

10. (a) A person of military age liable to report for regular service shall belong to the Regular Forces of the Defence Army of Israel from the time fixed by order for his so reporting; if he fails to report without sufficient excuse, he shall be deemed to have left the service without permission at such time.

(b) A person of military age liable to report for reserve service shall be deemed to be on service from the time fixed by order, for his so reporting; if he fails to report, without sufficient excuse, he shall be deemed to have left the service without permission at such time.

11. (a) Where the Minister of Defence is satisfied that a particular ordinary resident does not intend to settle within the territory in which the law of the State of Israel applies, he may, by certificate under his hand, exempt such person from the obligations imposed by this Law upon an ordinary resident.

(b) The following persons shall be exempt from the obligation of defence service:

(1) the mother of a child;

(2) a pregnant woman.

(c) A married woman shall be exempt from the obligation of regular service.

(d) A female person of military age who has declared that reasons of conscience or religious convictions prevent her from serving on defence service, shall, in such manner as shall be prescribed by regulations, be exempted from the obligation of defence service.

September 15, 1949

THE KNESSET VOTE JUNE 13, 1950 FOR A CONSTITUTION BY EVOLUTION

The First Knesset delegates the Constitution, Legislation, and Juridical Committee to prepare a draft constitution for the State.

The constitution shall be constructed article by article in such a manner that each of them shall in itself constitute a fundamental law.

Each article shall be brought before the Knesset as the Committee completes its work, and all the articles together shall comprise the State Constitution.

June 13, 1950

WOMEN'S EQUAL RIGHTS LAW, 5711–1951

1. A man and a woman shall have equal status with regard to any legal proceeding; any provision of law which discriminates, with regard to any legal proceeding, against women as women, shall be of no effect.

2. A married woman shall be fully competent to own and deal with property as if she were unmarried; her rights in property acquired before her marriage shall not be affected by her marriage.

3. (a) Both parents are the natural guardians of their children; where one parent dies, the survivor shall be the natural guardian.

(b) The provisions of subsection (a) shall not derogate from the power of a competent court or tribunal to deal with matters concerning the guardianship over the persons or property of children, having regard only to the interest of the children.

4. (a) Notwithstanding anything contained in any other law, rights in an estate, being mulk land or movable property, shall be determined in accordance with the provisions of the Second Schedule to the Succession Ordinance.

(b) The provisions of subsection (a) shall apply to any estate the order for the distribution of which is made after the coming into force of this Law, even if the deceased died before such coming into force.

(c) The provisions of subsection (a) do not apply to such items of an estate as are disposed of by will.

5. This Law shall not affect any legal prohibition or permission relating to marriage or divorce.

6. This Law shall not derogate from any provision of law protecting women as women.

7. All courts shall act in accordance with this Law; a tribunal competent to deal with matters of personal status shall likewise act in accordance therewith, unless all the parties are eighteen years of age or over and have consented before the tribunal, of their own free will, to have their case tried according to the laws of their community.

8. The Criminal Code Ordinance, 1936, shall be amended as follows:

(a) Paragraph (c) of the proviso to section 181 is repealed;

(b) the following section shall be inserted after section 181:

181A. Where the husband dissolves the marriage against the will of the wife without a judgment of a competent court or tribunal ordering the wife to dissolve the marriage, the husband is guilty of a felony and shall be liable to imprisonment for a term not exceeding five years.

9. The Minister of Justice is charged with the implementation of this Law.

July 26, 1951

STATE PRESIDENT (TENURE) LAW, 5712–1952

1. The President of the State is elected by the Knesseth.

2. The term of office of the President is five years from the day on which he assumes his functions.

3. The election of the President shall take place not earlier than ninety days and not later than thirty days before the expiration of the term of office of the preceding President;

if the tenure of the preceding President terminates before the expiration of the term fixed in section 2, the election shall take place within thirty days from the day of the termination of such tenure.

4. (a) The Chairman of the Knesseth shall fix a day, within the period prescribed in section 3, for the election of the President and shall give notice thereof in writing to all members of the Knesseth at least twenty days in advance.

(b) When the day of the election has been fixed, ten or more members of the Knesseth may propose a candidate for the presidency; the proposal shall be in writing and shall be submitted to the Chairman of the Knesseth not later than ten days before the day of the election, together with the consent of the candidate either in writing or by telegram.

(c) No member of the Knesseth shall sponsor the proposal of more than one candidate.

(d) The Chairman of the Knesseth shall notify all the members of the Knesseth in writing, not later than seven days before the day of the election, of each proposed candidate and of the names of the members of the Knesseth sponsoring him, and he shall also announce the proposed candidates at a meeting of the Knesseth.

5. (a) The election of the President shall take place by secret ballot at a meeting, or at consecutive meetings, of the Knesseth, devoted solely to this purpose.

(b) A candidate who receives a majority of votes of all the members of the Knesseth at the first ballot is elected. If no candidate receives a majority of votes as aforesaid at the first ballot, a second ballot shall be held, and a candidate who receives a majority of votes of all the members of the Knesseth at the second ballot is elected. If no candidate receives a majority of votes as aforesaid at the second ballot, voting shall continue, and a candidate who at a subsequent ballot receives a majority of votes of the members participating therein is elected.

6. As soon as possible after his election, the President-elect shall make and sign before the Knesseth the following declaration of allegiance:

> "I pledge myself to bear allegiance to the State of Israel and to its Laws and faithfully to carry out my functions as President of the State."

If the House Committee finds that owing to special circumstances the declaration cannot be made before the Knesseth, it shall determine before whom it shall be made.

7. The President shall assume his functions after his declaration of allegiance upon the expiration of the term of office of the preceding President; if the tenure of the preceding President terminates before the expiration of the term fixed in section 2, the President shall assume his functions on his declaration of allegiance.

8. (a) A member of the Knesseth who has been elected President shall cease to be a member of the Knesseth.

(b) Save with the sanction of the House Committee, the President shall hold no office, and shall carry out no functions, other than his office and functions as President.

(c) The President is exempt from all compulsory service.

9. (a) The President shall not be called to account before any court or tribunal in respect of a matter relating to his functions or powers; this immunity shall continue after he has ceased to be President.

(b) No legal action shall be taken against the President during his tenure of office.

(c) If the President is required to give evidence, his evidence shall be given at a time and place fixed with his sanction.

(d) The President's term of office shall not be taken into account in calculating the period of prescription of any legal proceeding to which he is a party.

10. The President shall not leave the territory of the State without the sanction of the Government.

11. The President may resign by submitting a letter of resignation to the Chairman of the Knesseth.

12. (a) The Knesseth may depose the President if it considers that he is unworthy of his office owing to conduct unbecoming to his status as President.

(b) The Knesseth shall not depose the President except by a decision taken by a three-quarters majority of all its members upon a proposal of the House Committee, which shall have been decided upon by a three-quarters majority of all the members of the Committee following a complaint brought before it by at least ten members of the Knesseth.

(c) The House Committee shall not propose the deposition of the President before he has been given an opportunity to refute the complaint in accordance with a procedure to be laid down by the Committee; and the Knesseth shall not decide to depose the President before he has been given an opportunity to state his case.

(d) The President is entitled to be represented before the Knesseth and before the House Committee by his representative, provided that a member of the Knesseth shall not act as representative of the President; but the Knesseth or the House Committee may require the attendance of the President before the Knesseth during its deliberations under this section.

(e) The deliberations of the Knesseth under this section shall be held at meetings of the Knesseth devoted solely to this purpose, after notice has been given in the manner specified in section 4(a).

13. The Knesseth may, by a decision taken by a three-quarters majority of its members upon a proposal of the House Committee decided upon by a three-quarters majority of its members, decide that for reasons of health the President is permanently unable to carry out his functions; the President's tenure shall terminate on the day on which such a decision is taken.

14. (a) In any of the following cases, the Chairman of the Knesseth shall, for the period specified in respect of each case, be Acting President of the State and as such shall carry out the functions and exercise the powers vested in the President by law:

(1) when the President has left the territory of the State–from the time of his departure until his return;

(2) when the House Committee, by a three-quarters majority, has decided that for reasons of health, the President is temporarily unable to carry out his functions–until the expiration of the period fixed by the Committee in its decision or until it decides, in accordance with a communication from the President, that he is no longer unable to carry out his functions.

(b) The House Committee shall not, in a decision under section (a)(2), fix a period exceeding four months, and it shall not, save with the approval of the Knesseth, extend the period fixed by it by more than four additional months.

15. When the President's tenure terminates, either at or before the appointed time, then, so long as the new President has not yet assumed his functions, the Chairman of the Knesseth shall be interim President of the State and as such shall carry out the functions and exercise the powers vested in the President by law.

16. The following shall be announced by notice in *Reshumoth:*

(1) the President's assumption of his functions;

(2) the termination of the President's tenure before the expiration of the period fixed in section 2;

(3) the beginning and end of the tenure of the Chairman of the Knesseth as Acting President under section 14.

17. (a) Sections 3, 4 and 5 of the Transition Law, 5709–1949, are repealed.

(b) The President elected by the Second Knesseth on the 20th Cheshvan, 5712 (19th November, 1951), shall be deemed to have been elected under this Law.

December 5, 1951

NATIONALITY LAW, 5712–1952

Part One: Acquisition of Nationality

1. Israel nationality is acquired—

by return (section 2),
by residence in Israel (section 3),
by birth (section 4), or
by naturalisation (sections 5 to 9).

There shall be no Israel nationality save under this Law.

2. (a) Every *'oleh* under the Law of Return, 5710–1950, shall become an Israel national.

(b) Israel nationality by return is acquired—

(1) by a person who came as an *'oleh* into, or was born in, the country before the establishment of the State—with effect from the day of the establishment of the State;

(2) by a person having come to Israel as an *'oleh* after the establishment of the State—with effect from the day of his *'alyiah;*

(3) by a person born in Israel after the establishment of the State—with effect from the day of his birth;

(4) by a person who has received an *'oleh's* certificate under section 3 of the Law of Return, 5710–1950—with effect from the day of the issue of the certificate.

(c) This section does not apply—

(1) to a person having ceased to be an inhabitant of Israel before the coming into force of this Law;

(2) to a person of full age who, immediately before the day of the coming into force of this Law or, if he comes to Israel as an *'oleh* thereafter, immediately before the day of his *'aliyah* or the day of the issue of his *'oleh*'s certificate is a foreign national and who, on or before such day, declares that he does not desire to become an Israel national.

(3) to a minor whose parents have made a declaration under paragraph (2) and included him therein.

3. (a) A person who, immediately before the establishment of the State, was a Palestinian citizen and who does not become an Israel national under section 2, shall become an Israel national with effect from the day of the establishment of the State if—

(1) he was registered on the 4th Adar, 5712 (1st March, 1952) as an inhabitant under the Registration of Inhabitants Ordinance, 5709–1949; and

(2) he is an inhabitant of Israel on the day of the coming into force of this Law; and

(3) he was in Israel, or in an area which became Israel territory after the establishment of the State, from the day of the establishment of the State to the day of the coming into force of this Law, or entered Israel legally during that period.

(b) A person born after the establishment of the State, who is an inhabitant of Israel on the day of the coming into force of this Law, and whose father or mother becomes an Israel national under subsection (a), shall become an Israel national with effect from the day of his birth.

4. A person born while his father or mother is an Israel national shall be an Israel national by birth; where a person is born after his father's death, it shall be sufficient that his father was an Israel national at the time of his death.

5. (a) A person of full age, not being an Israel national, may obtain Israel nationality by naturalisation if—

(1) he is in Israel; and

(2) he has been in Israel for three years out of the five years preceding the day of the submission of his application; and

(3) he is entitled to reside in Israel permanently; and

(4) he has settled, or intends to settle, in Israel; and

(5) he has some knowledge of the Hebrew language; and

(6) he has renounced his prior nationality or has proved that he will cease to be a foreign national upon becoming an Israel national.

(b) Where a person has applied for naturalisation and he meets the requirements of subsection (a), the Minister of the Interior, if he thinks fit to do so, shall grant him Israel nationality by issue of a certificate of naturalisation.

(c) Prior to the grant of nationality, the applicant shall make the following declaration:

"I declare that I will be a loyal national of the State of Israel."

(d) Nationality is acquired on the day of declaration.

6. (a)(1) A person who has served in the regular service of the Defence Army of Israel or who after the 16th Kislev, 5708 (29th November, 1947), has served in some other service which the Minister of Defence, by declaration published in *Reshumoth,* has declared to be military service for the purposes of this section, and who has been duly discharged from such service; and

(2) a person who has lost a son or daughter in such service,

are exempt from the requirements of section 5(a), except the requirement of section 5(a)(4).

(b) A person applying for naturalisation after having made a declaration under section 2(c)(2) is exempt from the requirement of section 5(a)(2).

(c) A person who immediately before the establishment of the State was a Palestinian citizen is exempt from the requirement of section 5(a)(5).

(d) The Minister of the Interior may exempt an applicant from all or any of the requirements of section 5(a)(1), (2), (5) and (6) if there exists in his opinion a special reason justifying such exemption.

7. The spouse of a person who is an Israel national or who has applied for Israel nationality and meets or is exempt from the requirements of section 5(a) may obtain Israel nationality by naturalisation even if she or he is a minor or does not meet the requirements of section 5(a).

8. Naturalisation confers Israel nationality also upon the minor children of the naturalised person.

9. (a) Where a minor, not being an Israel national, is an inhabitant of Israel, and his parents are not in Israel or have

died or are unknown, the Minister of the Interior, on such conditions and with effect from such day he may think fit, may grant him Israel nationality by the issue of a certificate of naturalisation.

(b) Nationality may be granted as aforesaid upon the application of the father or mother of the minor or, if they have died or are unable to apply, upon the application of the guardian or person in charge of the minor.

PART TWO: LOSS OF NATIONALITY

10. (a) An Israel national of full age, not being an inhabitant of Israel, may declare that he desires to renounce his Israel nationality; such renunciation is subject to the consent of the Minister of the Interior; the declarant's Israel nationality terminates on the day fixed by the Minister.

(b) The Israel nationality of a minor, not being an inhabitant of Israel, terminates upon his parents' renouncing their Israel nationality; it does not terminate so long as one of his parents remains an Israel national.

11. (a) Where a person, having acquired Israel nationality by naturalisation,

(1) has done so on the basis of false particulars; or

(2) has been abroad for seven consecutive years and has no effective connection with Israel, and has failed to prove that his effective connection with Israel was severed otherwise than by his own volition; or

(3) has committed an act of disloyalty towards the State of Israel,

a District Court may, upon the application of the Minister of the Interior, revoke such person's naturalisation.

(b) The Court may, upon such application, rule that the revocation shall apply also to such children of the naturalised person as acquired Israel nationality by virtue of his naturalisation and are resident abroad.

(c) Israel nationality terminates on the day on which the judgment revoking naturalisation ceases to be appealable or on such later day as the Court may fix.

12. Loss of Israel nationality does not relieve the loser of a liability arising out of such nationality and created before its loss.

Part Three: Further Provisions

13. In this Law—

"of full age" means of the age of eighteen years or over;

"minor" means a person under eighteen years of age;

"child" includes an adopted child, and "parents" include adoptive parents;

"foreign nationality" includes foreign citizenship, and "foreign national" includes a foreign citizen, but does not include a Palestinian citizen.

14. (a) Save for the purposes of naturalisation, acquisition of Israel nationality is not conditional upon renunciation of a prior nationality.

(b) An Israel national who is also a foreign national shall, for the purposes of Israel law, be considered as an Israel national.

(c) An inhabitant of Israel residing abroad shall, for the purposes of this Law, be considered as an inhabitant of Israel so long as he has not settled abroad.

15. An Israel national may obtain from the Minister of the Interior a certificate attesting to his Israel nationality.

16. A person who knowingly gives false particulars as to a matter affecting his own or another person's acquisition or loss

of Israel nationality is liable to imprisonment for a term not exceeding six months or to a fine not exceeding five hundred pounds, or to both such penalties.

17. (a) The Minister of the Interior is charged with the implementation of this Law and may make regulations as to any matter relating to its implementation, including the payment of fees and exemption from the payment thereof.

(b) The Minister of Justice may make regulations as to proceedings in District Courts under this Law, including appeals from decisions of such Courts.

18. (a) The Palestinian Citizenship Orders, 1925-42, are repealed with effect from the day of the establishment of the State.

(b) Any reference in any provision of law to Palestinian citizenship or Palestinian citizens shall henceforth be read as a reference to Israel nationality or Israel nationals.

(c) Any act done in the period between the establishment of the State and the day of the coming into force of this Law shall be deemed to be valid if it would have been valid had this Law been in force at the time it was done.

19. (a) This Law shall come into force on the 21st Tammuz, 5712 (14th July, 1952).

(b) Even before that day, the Minister of the Interior may make regulations as to declarations under section 2(c)(2).

April 8, 1952

ENTRY INTO ISRAEL LAW, 5712–1952

PART ONE: PERMISSION OF ENTRY AND RESIDENCE

1. The entry of a person, other than an Israel national or an *oleh* under the Law of the Return, 5710–1950, into Israel shall be by visa, and his residence in Israel shall be by permit of residence, under this Law.

2. The Minister of the Interior may grant—

(1) a visa and permit of transitory residence (up to 5 days);

(2) a visa and visitor's permit of residence (up to 3 months);

(3) a visa and permit of temporary residence (up to 3 years);

(4) a visa and permit of permanent residence.

3. The Minister of the Interior may extend—

(1) a permit of transitory residence, provided that the aggregate period of extensions shall not exceed ten days;

(2) a visitor's permit of residence, provided that the aggregate period of extensions shall not exceed two years;

(3) a permit of temporary residence, provided that the period of any extension shall not exceed two years.

4. The Minister of the Interior may substitute for a permit of residence of a shorter-term category a permit of residence of a longer-term category or a permit of permanent residence.

5. The Minister of the Interior may grant a return visa to a person who, being permitted to reside in Israel permanently—

(1) wishes to leave Israel with the intention of returning; or

(2) is abroad and wishes to return to Israel.

6. The Minister of the Interior may—

(1) prescribe conditions for the grant of a visa and for the grant, extension or substitution of a permit of residence;

(2) prescribe, in a visa or permit of residence, conditions upon the fulfilment of which the validity of such visa or permit shall depend.

PART TWO: PROCEDURE OF ENTRY

7. No person shall enter Israel otherwise than at one of the frontier stations prescribed by the Minister of the Interior by order published in *Reshumot.*

8. (a) The master of any ship or the person in charge of any aircraft, train, motorcar or other means of transportation which has come to Israel shall deliver to a frontier control officer, on his demand, a list of the persons in such means of transportation, including the personnel thereof; the list shall contain the particulars prescribed by the Minister of the Interior by regulations under this Law.

(b) A frontier control officer may enter and carry out an inspection in any means of transportation which has come to Israel; and any person therein, including any member of the personnel thereof, shall produce to such frontier control officer, on his demand, any documents, and shall give him any information, relevant to the implementation of this Law.

9. Where a person comes to Israel and wishes to enter, a frontier control officer may delay his entry until it has been ascertained whether he is permitted to enter, and he may indicate a place where such person shall stay until completion of such ascertainment or until his departure from Israel.

10. (a) Where a person comes to Israel and it is found that he is not permitted to enter, the Minister of the Interior may remove him from Israel.

(b) A frontier control officer may detain such a person, in such place and manner as the Minister of the Interior may prescribe, until his departure or removal from Israel.

(c) The master of any ship or the person in charge of any aircraft, train, motorcar or other means of transportation which has come to Israel shall, on the demand of a frontier control officer, take out of Israel any person who has arrived by that means of transportation with the intention of entering Israel, if it has been found that he is not permitted to enter.

PART THREE: MISCELLANEOUS PROVISIONS

11. (a) The Minister of the Interior may at his discretion—

(1) cancel any visa granted under this Law, either before or on the arrival of the visa holder in Israel;

(2) cancel any permit of residence granted under this Law.

(b) The Minister of the Interior may cancel any *oleh*'s visa or *oleh*'s certificate granted under the Law of the Return, 5710—1950, if it has been obtained by the supply of false information.

12. Any person who—

(1) enters or resides in Israel in contravention of the law; or

(2) supplies false information in order to obtain, for himself or for another, a visa for or permit of residence in Israel; or

(3) infringes any of the conditions prescribed in the visa or permit of residence granted him under this law; or

(4) contravenes any other provision of this Law or any regulations made thereunder, is liable to imprisonment for a term not exceeding three months or to a fine not exceeding three hundred pounds or to both such penalties.

13. (a) In respect of a person other than an Israel national or an *oleh* under the Law of the Return, 5710—1950, the Minister of the Interior may issue an order of deportation if such person is in Israel without a permit of residence.

(b) A person in respect of whom an order of deportation has been issued shall leave Israel and shall not return so long as the order of deportation has not been cancelled.

(c) Where an order of deportation has been issued in respect of any person, a frontier control officer or police officer may arrest him and detain him in such place and manner as the Minister of the Interior may prescribe, until his departure or deportation from Israel.

(d) The Minister of the Interior may direct that an order of deportation shall be carried out at the expense of the person in respect of whom it has been issued.

14. The Minister of the Interior may make regulations as to any matter relating to the implementation of this Law, including, *inter alia,* regulations as to the following:

(1) categories of persons who shall be disqualified for the receipt of a visa or permit of residence under this Law;

(2) conditions to be fulfilled prior to the grant of a visa, or the grant, extension or substitution of a permit of residence, under this Law;

(3) the medical examination, medical treatment and sanitary inspection of persons entering Israel, and the disinfection of their clothing and effects;

(4) fees payable in respect of the grant of a visa and the grant, extension or substitution of a permit of residence.

15. (a) The Minister of the Interior is charged with the implementation of this Law.

(b) The Minister of the Interior may appoint frontier control officers for the purposes of this Law; notice of such appointments shall be published in *Reshumot.*

16. (a) The Minister of the Interior may delegate to another person all or any of his powers under this Law, except the

power to make regulations; notice of any such delegation of powers shall be published in *Reshumot.*

(b) A person who considers himself aggrieved by a decision under section 11 or 13, made in exercise of a power delegated by the Minister, may apply to the Minister for a final decision.

17. (a) This Law shall not apply to a person who comes to Israel by virtue of a diplomatic or service visa.

(b) The Minister of the Interior, after consultation with the Home Affairs Committee of the Knesset, may, by order published in *Reshumot,* exempt additional categories of persons, either completely or with restrictions, from all or any of the provisions of this Law.

(c) The Minister of the Interior may permit a passenger in transit, who has arrived in Israel by ship or aircraft, to stay in Israel without a visa or permit of residence until the departure of such ship or aircraft.

18. (a) This Law shall apply to a person who enters Israel after the coming into force thereof and to the residence of such a person in Israel.

(b) With regard to a person who entered Israel prior to the coming into force of this Law, the position shall be the same as it would have been had this Law not been enacted.

(c) Where any person, on the 16th Kislev, 5708 (29th November, 1947), was an inhabitant of the area which has become Israel territory, and he left such area prior to that date, and he applies, within two years from the coming into force of this Law, for permission to return to Israel, the Minister of the Interior may grant him a visa for that purpose.

19. The Immigration Ordinance, 1941, is hereby repealed. The Immigration Rules set out in the Schedule to the said Ordinance, as well as regulations, orders and notices made or given, and visas, permits and certificates granted thereunder

shall have effect as if they had been made, given or granted under this Law.

September 5, 1952

STATE EDUCATION LAW, 5713–1953
(Excerpts)

1. In this Law—

"State education" means education provided by the State on the basis of the curriculum, without attachment to a party or communal body or any other organisation outside the Government, and under the supervision of the Minister or a person authorised by him in that behalf;

"religious State education" means State education, with the distinction that its institutions are religious as to their way of life, curriculum, teachers and inspectors;

"the curriculum" means a curriculum prescribed by the Minister for the official educational institutions with a view to attaining the object stated in section 2, and includes the "basic programme" to be prescribed by the Minister as an obligatory programme for every such institution;

"State-educational institution" means an official educational institution in which State education is provided, but does not include a religious State-educational institution;

"religious State-educational institution" means an institution in which religious State education is provided;

"supplementary programme" means a part of the curriculum to be prescribed or approved by the Minister under this Law and comprising not more than twenty-five per cent of the lesson hours in an official educational institution; supplementary programme for a religious State-educational institution means a supplementary programme comprising the study of the written and oral religious law and aimed at a religious way of life, and includes religious observance and a religious atmosphere within the institution;

"pupil" means a child or an adolescent;

The other terms have the same meaning as in the Compulsory Education Law, 5709–1949 (hereinafter: "the Compulsory Education Law").

2. The object of State education is to base elementary education in the State on the values of Jewish culture and the achievements of science, on love of the homeland and loyalty to the State and the Jewish people, on practice in agricultural work and handicraft, on *chalutzic* (pioneer) training, and on striving for a society built on freedom, equality, tolerance, mutual assistance and love of mankind.

3. From the school year 5714 onwards, State education shall be introduced in every official educational institution; in an official educational institution which in the school year 5713 belonged to the Mizrachi trend or the Agudat Israel trend or the religious section of the Labour trend, religious State education shall be introduced.

4. The Minister shall prescribe the curriculum of every official educational institution; in non-Jewish educational institutions, the curriculum shall be adapted to the special conditions thereof.

5. The Minister may prescribe for every official educational institution a supplementary programme to be introduced therein —either one programme for the whole institution or different programmes for different or parallel classes; in the case of a religious State-educational institution, one of the supplementary programmes for a religious State-educational institution shall be prescribed.

6. On the demand of the parents of pupils in an educational institution, the Minister may, on conditions prescribed by regulations, approve for that institution a supplementary programme other than that prescribed under section 5.

7. The Minister shall not exercise his power under section 6 if he is satisfied that another supplementary programme will

involve extra expenditure; provided that if the extra expenditure devolves on a local education authority, he may exercise the said power with the consent of that authority.

8. The Minister may, on conditions prescribed by regulations, approve for an official educational institution, on the demand of parents of pupils in that institution, a programme for hours additional to the hours prescribed in the curriculum, provided that all the expenditure involved in implementing the additional programme shall be borne by the parents of the pupils educated thereunder or by the local education authority which has undertaken to defray it.

9. The Minister may, for experimental purposes, introduce in a particular official educational institution a curriculum not in accordance with the provisions of this Law; provided that he shall give advance notice of its introduction, in a manner prescribed by regulations, before the beginning of the registration under section 20, and provided further that such an institution shall not be designated as the only nearby institution in respect of pupils living in its vicinity.

10. (a) The Minister may order a local education authority, or several local education authorities, to amalgamate official educational institutions situated within its or their area or areas; however, he shall not order the amalgamation of a State-educational institution with a religious State-educational institution.

(b) The Minister shall not order the amalgamation of official educational institutions situated in the areas of two or more local education authorities unless he has given advance notice in writing to the local education authorities concerned, and unless they have been given an opportunity to express their opposition, if any, to the Minister.

11. The Minister may, by regulations, prescribe a procedure and conditions for the declaration of non-official institutions as recognised educational institutions, the introduction therein of

the basic programme, the management and supervision thereof and the assistance of the State towards their budgets, if and to the extent that the Minister decides on such assistance.

12. There shall be established a Committee on Matters of Education (hereinafter: "Education Committee"), the number of the members of which shall not be less than fifteen. The members of the Committee shall be appointed by the Minister with the approval of the Government, each for a period of four years. Those appointed shall be persons active in the field of education, employees of the Ministry of Education and Culture, whose number shall not exceed 25 per cent of the total membership of the Committee, and candidates of local authorities, the institutions of higher learning and the Teachers' Federation from lists submitted to the Minister upon his request.

13. There shall be established a Council for Religious State Education; the members of the Council shall be appointed by the Minister with the approval of the Government, each for a period of four years. Two members shall be representatives of the Minister, six shall be appointed from a list of twelve candidates proposed by the Minister of Religious Affairs, three from a list of at least candidates proposed, in accordance with regulations, by teachers' organizations representing the religious teachers, and three from among the religious members of the Education Committee.

August 20, 1953

NATIONAL SERVICE LAW, 5713–1953

1. In this Law—

"person eligible for service" means a woman who has been exempted from defence service under section 11(d) of the Defence Service Law, 5709–1949, and who is of any age from 18 to 26 years inclusive;

"national service" means any of the following:

(1) service in agricultural work or in agricultural training, either in a religious agricultural settlement or in a religious agricultural institution;

(2) labour service for the Defence Army of Israel, or other labour service for the security of the State;

(3) service in an immigrants' camp, a *ma'bara* (immigrants' transitional settlement), an educational or social welfare institution or an institution for medical care;

(4) labour service in another institution of the State, defined by the Minister as an institution for the purpose of this Law;

"the Minister" means the member of the Government on whom the Government has conferred the power to implement this law.

2. A person eligible for service is liable to national service for a period of 24 months.

3. The Minister shall appoint inspectors for the purpose of this Law. The appointment may be general or restricted, and notice thereof shall be published in *Reshumot.*

4. (1) The nature, conditions, place and time of national service shall be prescribed by an inspector by order.

(2) The kind of service within the framework of the national service shall be prescribed by the inspector having regard to the preference of the person eligible for service.

5. An order regulating matters of discipline shall be made only by an inspector whose appointment is general.

6. An inspector shall make an order under section 4 only in respect of a person eligible for service who has been found medically fit for national service. The provisions of the Defence Ser-

vice Law, 5709—1949, relating to the determination of fitness for defence service shall apply, with adaptations to be prescribed by regulations, to the determination of fitness for national service.

7. The calculation of age for the purpose of this Law shall be made in accordance with the provisions of the Defence Service Law, 5709—1949, relating to the calculation of age.

8. A person eligible for service exempted from defence service on religious grounds shall be assured during her national service of an opportunity to maintain a religious way of life in accordance with rules to be prescribed by regulations.

9. A person eligible for service shall perform on national service any task lawfully assigned to her, and shall obey any lawful direction given her by her superior at the time of her service.

10. For the purpose of the Workmen's Compensation Ordinance 1947, and of any other law providing for compulsory insurance against labour injuries, a person eligible for service shall, while on national service, be deemed to be a workman; and the person for whom she works shall be deemed to be her employer.

11. The duties of a person for whom a person eligible for service works in connection with her national service shall be prescribed by an inspector by order.

12. A married woman is exempt from national service.

In this section, "married woman" means also the mother of a child, a pregnant woman and a woman who has married during the period of her national service.

13. The Minister shall appoint general or special boards for national service which shall be authorized to grant relief from the duty of national service, or to postpone the service, for family, educational or economic reasons or for reasons connected with a family's special way of life. Application to a board shall

not suspend liability to service unless the board otherwise orders.

14. The Minister may grant relief from the duty of national service for any of the reasons enumerated in section 13, either on his own motion or upon an objection to a decision of a board for national service.

15. An order under this Law may be personal or to a particular class of persons and does not require publication in *Reshumot*. The order binds the person to whom it relates from the time at which it comes to his or her knowledge.

16. An order sent by registered post to the permanent residential address of the person to whom it relates is considered to have come to the knowledge of such person at the expiration of 72 hours from the time at which it was delivered to the post office for dispatch.

17. A person who—

(1) does not fulfil a duty imposed under this Law; or

(2) refuses to obey, or is negligent in carrying out, a direction lawfully given, is liable to imprisonment for a term of one year or to a fine of one thousand pounds or to both such penalties, or where the person did not fulfil a duty imposed under this Law with intent to evade national service, imprisonment for a term of three years.

18. Where an order has been made under this Law imposing on a person eligible for service a duty to be fulfilled at a time prescribed in the order, and she has not fulfilled the duty at such time, the order shall remain in force with regard to her until she fulfils the duty; the provision of this section does not affect the criminal liability of a person eligible for service for non-fulfilment of a duty at the time prescribed in an order, and her conviction of non-fulfilment of a duty imposed on her does not relieve her from that duty.

19. The Minister may make regulations as to any matter relating to the implementation of this Law.

20. This Law does not apply to a person eligible for service who was exempted from defence service, whether before or after the coming into force of this Law, on an application submitted to an exemption board before the 1st Av, 5713 (13th July, 1953).

September 4, 1953

RABBINICAL COURTS JURISDICTION (MARRIAGE AND DIVORCE) LAW, 5713–1953

1. Matters of marriage and divorce of Jews in Israel, being nationals or residents of the State, shall be under the exclusive jurisdiction of rabbinical courts.

2. Marriages and divorces of Jews shall be performed in Israel in accordance with Jewish religious law.

3. Where a suit for divorce between Jews has been filed in a rabbinical court, whether by the wife or by the husband, a rabbinical court shall have exclusive jurisdiction in any matter connected with such suit, including maintenance for the wife and for the children of the couple.

4. Where a Jewish wife sues her Jewish husband or his estate for maintenance in a rabbinical court, otherwise than in connection with divorce, the plea of the defendant that a rabbinical court has no jurisdiction in the matter shall not be heard.

5. Where a woman sues her deceased husband's brother for *chalitza* in a rabbinical court, the rabbinical court shall have exclusive jurisdiction in the matter, also as regards maintenance for the woman until the day on which *chalitza* is given.

6. Where a rabbinical court, by final judgment, has ordered that a husband be compelled to grant his wife a letter of divorce

or that a wife be compelled to accept a letter of divorce from her husband, a district court may, upon expiration of six months from the day of the making of the order, on the application of the Attorney General, compel compliance with the order by imprisonment.

7. Where a rabbinical court, by final judgment, has ordered that a man be compelled to give his brother's widow *chalitza,* a district court may, upon expiration of three months from the day of the making of the order, on application of the Attorney General, compel compliance with the order by imprisonment.

8. For the purpose of sections 6 and 7, a judgment shall be regarded as final when it is no longer appealable.

9. In matters of personal status of Jews, as specified in article 51 of the Palestine Orders in Council, 1922 to 1947, or in the Succession Ordinance, in which a rabbinical court has not exclusive jurisdiction under this Law, a rabbinical court shall have jurisdiction after all parties concerned have expressed their consent thereto.

10. A judgment given by a rabbinical court after the establishment of the State and before the coming into force of this Law, after the case had been heard in the presence of the litigants, and which would have been validly given had this Law been in force at the time, shall be deemed to have been validly given.

11. The Minister of Religious Affairs is charged with the implementation of this Law.

September 4th, 1953

PENAL LAW REVISION (ABOLITION OF THE DEATH PENALTY FOR MURDER) LAW, 5714–1954

1. Where a person has been convicted of murder, the Court shall impose the penalty of imprisonment for life, and only that penalty.

2. Section 215 of the Criminal Code Ordinance, 1936, shall no longer be applied, except where a person has been convicted of murder under section 2(f) of the Nazis and Nazi Collaborators (Punishment) Law, 5710–1950.

3. A person who has been sentenced to death before the coming into force of this Law shall be deemed to have been sentenced to imprisonment for life.

February 24, 1954

GLOSSARY

Agudat Israel: an ultra-orthodox party
Aliyah: immigration to Israel
Aschulta d'Geula: beginning of the redemption
Ashkenazi: descended from Yiddish-speaking Jews

Chaver: (a friend) a member of a party or organization

Dayan: rabbinical judge
Diaspora: dispersion of Jews outside Israel
Divrei ha-Knesset: Parliament Record

Eretz Israel: Land of Israel

Halakha: Jewish religious-traditional law
Haoved Hadadi: Religious Workingman (wing of Mapai)
Haskalah: Enlightenment
Herut: Freedom Movement, a rightist party
Histadruth: Histadruth ha-Klalit shel ha-Ovdim Haivrim b'Eretz Yisrael, the abbreviation for the General Federation of Labor in Israel

Iton Rishmi: The Official Gazette during the Provisional Government

Jewish Agency: the organization of Zionists and non-Zionists established in 1929 to advise the British Government on Palestine

Kasher: ritually prepared food
Kibbutz: a communal farm
Knesset: Parliament of Israel
Knesset Israel: National Jewish Community in the years of the Mandate
Kulturkampf: struggle around cultural issues

Ma'bara: immigrants' transitional settlement
Mapai: Mifleget Poalei Eretz Israel, Party of the Workers of the Land of Israel

Mapam: Mifleget ha-Poalim ha-Meuchedet, the United Workers Party

Meah She'arim: an ultra-orthodox quarter of Jerusalem, settled by followers of Neturei Karta

Mizrahi: a religious middle-class party, merged with Hapoel Hamizrahi in the National Religious Front

Moshav: a cooperative village

Neturei Karta: "guardians" of the city, an ultra-religious Jewish group concentrated in Meah She'arim, Jerusalem

Oleh: a Jew immigrating to Israel

Poalei Agudat Israel: the labor wing of the Agudat Israel

Reform Judaism: Jewish liberal theological trend

Reshumot: the Official Gazette since the First Knesset

Sanhedrin: High Rabbinical Assembly (during the second Temple)

Sephardi: descended from Spanish Jews

Sefer ha'Hukim: Statute Book of Legislation, a section of Reshumot

Shulhan Arukh: the code of orthodox Judaism

Torah: Pentateuch (the five books of Moses)

Va'ad Leumi: National Jewish Council in the years of the Mandate

Yemenite: descended from Yemen (South Arabic) Jews

Yishuv: the Jewish community in the years of the Mandate

BIBLIOGRAPHY

I. *Official Publications*

Divrei ha-Knesset [The Official Record of the Knesset Parliament], Vols. I-XXII. Jerusalem, Israel: Government Printer, 1949-1957.

Iton Rishmi [The Official Gazette during the tenure of the Provisional Government], Nos. 1-50. Hakirya, Israel: Government Printer, 1948-1949.

Moezath ha-Medina ha-Zmanith [The Official Record of the Provisional Council of State], Vols. I-II. Tel Aviv, Israel: Government Printer, 1948-1949.

Palestine Gazette [The Official Gazette of the Mandatory Government of Palestine]. Jerusalem, Palestine: Government of Palestine, 1936.

Sefer ha'Hukim [Book of Laws] (Section I on Principal Legislation of the Official Gazette since the inception of the Knesset), Nos. 1-265. Tel Aviv–Jerusalem, Israel: Government Printer, 1949-1958.

State of Israel Facts and Figures, 1954. Hakirya, Israel: Government Printer, 1954. Pp. 55.

State of Israel Government Yearbook, Vols. I-IX. Tel Aviv–Jerusalem, Israel: Government Printer, 1949-1957.

A Survey of Palestine, Vol. II. Jerusalem, Palestine: Government Printer, 1946. Pp. 535-1139.

United Nations Resolutions, 1947. Lake Success, New York: United Nations, September 16–November 29, 1947. Pp. 153.

Yalkut ha-Pirsumim [Section II of Government Notices of the Official Gazette since the inception of the Knesset], Nos. 1-619. Tel Aviv–Jerusalem, Israel: Government Printer, 1949-1958.

II. *Books and Pamphlets*

Baron, Salo Wittmayer. *A Social and Religious History of the Jews.* Vol. 1. New York: Columbia University Press, 1937. Pp. 377.

Buber, Martin. *Hasidism.* New York: Philosophical Library, 1948. Pp. 207.

Caro, Joseph. *Shulhan Arukh.* Vol. *Yorah Deah* [Teaching Knowledge]. Vilno: Widow Ram and Brothers, 1880. Pp. 531.

Cohen, Israel. *The Zionist Movement.* London, England: Frederick Muller Ltd., 1945. Pp. 352.

Davis, Helen Miller (ed.). *Constitutions, Laws, Treaties of States in the Near and Middle East.* Durham, N.C.: Duke University Press, 1953. Pp. 541.

De Gaury, Gerald. *The New State of Israel.* New York: Frederick A. Praeger, 1952. Pp. 260.

Documents Relating to the Palestine Problem. London, England: Jewish Agency for Palestine, 1945. Pp. 96.

Draft Constitution for Israel, The (*The Jewish Agency's Digest of Press and Events,* Supplement No. 12) Jerusalem, 1948. Pp. 19.

Drayton, Robert Harry (ed.). *The Laws of Palestine,* Vols. I-III. London, England: Government of Palestine, 1934. Pp. 2668.

Facts About Israel. New York: Israel Office of Information, 1957. Pp. 144.

Greenberg, Hayim (ed.). *Dath Israel u-Medinath Israel.* New York: World Zionist Organization, 1951.

Herzl, Theodor. *Der Yudenstaat.* Berlin, Germany: Yudisher Verlag, 1934. Pp. 96.

Hess, Moses. *Rome and Jerusalem.* Tel Aviv, Israel: Hozaah-Ivrith, 1935. Pp. 253.

Holy Bible (Hebrew and English). Trans. by Isaac Loeser. New York: Hebrew Publishing Co. Pp. 396.

Leybovitz, Yeshayahu. *Torah u'Mytzwoth Byzman Hazeh.* Tel Aviv, Israel: Masada, 5614. Pp. 173.

Ostrowski, Rabbi Moshe. *Irgun ha-Yishaw ha-Yehudi be-Eretz Israel.* Jerusalem, Israel: Rubin Mass, 1942. Pp. 111.

Pinsker, Leo. *Auto-Emancipation.* New York: Masada, Youth Zionist Organization of America, 1935. Pp. 31.

Seven Years of Israel Independence. New York: Israel Office of Information, April, 1955. Pp. 2.

State of Israel Facts and Figures, 1954, 1955, 1956. New York: Israel Office of Information, 1954, 1955, 1956. Pp. 77, 98, 112.

III. *Periodicals*

Jewish Frontier (New York), 1948-1955.
Jewish Horizon (Easton, Pa.), 1948-1955.
Igereth-Lagolah (Jerusalem, Israel).
Mizrahi Weg (New York).
Nation, The (New York).
Yavneh (Jerusalem–Tel Aviv, Israel), 1949-1953.
Zionist Newsletter (Jerusalem, Israel).
Zionist Record (Johannesburg, South Africa).

IV. *Newspapers*

Forward, A Jewish Daily (New York).
Jersualem Post [formerly the *Palestine Post*] (Jerusalem, Israel).
New York Times (New York).
Der Tog [The Day] (New York).

INDEX

N

O

P

R

S

T